A Chef's
AIR FRYER
COOKBOOK for BEGINNERS

DELICIOUSLY SIMPLE RECIPES FOR QUICK GOURMET MEALS: EXPERIENCE A MEDITERRANEAN TWIST FROM A CULINARY MAESTRO

BONUS: TWO MUST-HAVE GUIDES!

1. REVEALED: Chef Claudio's Top 15 Air Fryers: Tested, reviewed, and rated! Get the inside scoop on the 15 best-selling air fryers in the US. Chef Claudio's expert advice will help you choose the perfect one for your kitchen!

2. EXCLUSIVE: 200+ Foods Made Easy: Chef Claudio's Essential Air Fryer Cheat Sheet! Whether you own a Ninja, Cosori, or any other model, this detailed cheat sheet is your key to getting each dish right—every time! Exact cooking tips for perfect air frying.

Claudio Belloni

Table of Contents

PROLOGUE

Ah, the continual dance of tradition and innovation in the culinary world never ceases to both challenge and excite me, Claudio Belloni. My life, deeply rooted in the rich soils of Milan and nurtured by the salty breezes of the Ligurian Sea, has been a testament to the enduring power of traditional cooking methods. With a pestle and mortar, I have pounded out not only pesto but also a life's worth of culinary devotion, much like my beloved Uncle Pio once taught me.

Imagine my surprise, then, when my favorite niece, Elisabetta, a spirited young soul with a burgeoning passion for cooking much like my own in younger days, requested an air fryer for Christmas. An air fryer, of all things! This modern gadget, so alien to a chef who delights in the old ways, initially struck me as a harbinger of culinary compromise.

Elisabetta, with her bright eyes and eager heart, sees the world with a wonder that I cherish deeply. How could I deny her this wish? Thus, with a heart both curious and cautious, I embarked on a journey to understand this device. To my astonishment, I discovered not a soulless machine, but rather an ingenious tool capable of merging the oven and fryer into one, delivering delightful dishes with but a fraction of the oil traditionally used. My reservations began to wane as I envisioned the possibility of light, healthful meals prepared with speed yet retaining their gourmet allure.

Who then, would guide Elisabetta in unlocking the true potential of such a device? Amid the sea of existing manuals, none struck the right chord—each one lacking the warmth and personality that cooking, to me, must invariably possess. It became clear what I must do. If the wisdom of a lifetime spent by the stove was to be passed down, then it would be through my own words, my own recipes.

Thus, I set to work, crafting not just a manual but a gateway to Mediterranean delights through the lens of modern technology. This book, born out of a blend of necessity and love, aims to equip my dear Elisabetta—and indeed, all who cherish both health and flavor—with the skills to transform simple ingredients into splendid meals.

To my beloved readers in America and beyond, I extend this collection of recipes as a bridge between old-world charm and new-world efficiency. From my heart to your homes, may you savor each dish with as much joy as I found in creating them.

Salute to you, dear friends. May your kitchens be lively, your meals flavorful, and your gatherings merry. Enjoy these recipes with the same spirit of adventure and affection with which they were conceived. Cheers, and happy cooking with your air fryer!

Claudio

INTRODUCTION

Welcome to Air Frying

In the ever-evolving world of culinary arts, where the whispers of tradition blend seamlessly with the strides of innovation, the air fryer emerges as a symbol of modern convenience. As Chef Claudio Belloni, I have spent decades cherishing the slow simmer of a saucepan and the gentle heat of an oven, always preferring the traditional methods taught to me in the bustling kitchens of Genoa. Yet, even an old chef like myself cannot help but be drawn to the ingenious simplicity of air frying. This chapter is a heartfelt invitation to explore how this remarkable appliance can revolutionize your cooking—making it faster, healthier, and just as delicious, all while keeping the essence of Mediterranean flair alive in your dishes.

Understanding Air Fryers: Function and Mechanics

Imagine, if you will, a compact device that sits neatly on your countertop, promising to whip up your favorite dishes in a fraction of the time taken by conventional methods. An air fryer, dear friends, is not so much a fryer as it is a marvel of rapid air technology. At its heart lies a powerful heating element and a fan that circulates hot air at high speed, enveloping the food placed inside in a uniform heat that cooks it quickly and evenly.

This method, known as convection cooking, crisps your food exquisitely—a feat traditionally achieved through deep-frying in copious amounts of oil. However, the air fryer accomplishes this with just a tablespoon or less of oil, reducing fat content substantially and offering a healthier alternative that does not compromise on taste or texture. The result? Deliciously crispy vegetables, meats, and even pastries that maintain their moisture and flavor, all achieved with minimal effort and maximum efficiency.

By adjusting temperature and cooking time, you have complete control over the cooking process, whether you're preparing delicate fish, robust chicken thighs, or tender pastries. And worry not about space; this device is designed to fit well within the confines of a modern kitchen, requiring no more room than a standard microwave.

In embracing the air fryer, we take a step towards the future of cooking, combining the wisdom of traditional methods with the efficiency of modern technology. Let us journey through the benefits and wonders of air frying, and discover how it can transform the very way we think about preparing meals.

The Convenience and Health Benefits of Air Frying

As a chef who has always cherished the tactile joy of cooking—feeling the stir of a wooden spoon, the sizzle of olive oil in a hot pan—it might surprise you to hear me sing the praises of a machine like the air fryer. Yet, here I am, dear friends, marveling at how this modern appliance has simplified cooking without sacrificing the soul of the dish.

Convenience is paramount in today's fast-paced world. The air fryer heats up in a mere fraction of the time it takes an oven, making it an indispensable ally on busy evenings when time is of the essence. With its compact size, it sits comfortably on your countertop, always ready to tackle whatever recipe you throw its way. Whether it's crispy chicken wings for a family gathering or a quick vegetable side dish to accompany your pasta, the air fryer handles it with astonishing speed and efficiency.

Moreover, the health benefits of air frying cannot be overstated. In my younger days, indulging in the rich, oil-laden delights of Mediterranean cuisine came with few second thoughts. However, as the years have passed, I've grown to appreciate the importance of a balanced approach to eating. The air fryer allows us to enjoy our favorite fried foods with a significantly reduced amount of oil. This is not just beneficial for cutting calories—it also helps in reducing the intake of unhealthy fats, aligning our beloved Mediterranean dishes with a healthier lifestyle without compromising their integrity.

By using hot air to cook the food, the air fryer crisps the exterior to a perfect golden brown while keeping the inside moist and flavorful. This method retains the nutrients in your food better than traditional frying, which can often deplete the goodness from our fresh ingredients.

In embracing the air fryer, I've discovered a wonderful balance between the old and the new. It reassures me that we can uphold the traditions of our rich culinary past while making smart choices for our health and our time. This device is not just about convenience; it's about enriching our lives with meals that are both nourishing and delightful to the palate.

So, let us continue to gather around the table, sharing stories and laughter over dishes that are prepared with love, less oil, and a touch of modern ingenuity. After all, good food is not just about the ingredients we use but the love with which we prepare them.

Comparison of Air Frying to Traditional Frying Methods

Ah, the art of frying! There's something undeniably enchanting about the way a simple fry can transform the humblest ingredients into golden, crispy delights. As a young chef in the bustling kitchens of Genoa, I mastered the dance of deep frying, where olive oil was not just an ingredient but a liquid gold that brought life to dishes. Yet, as times change, so too do our methods. Now, as I explore the realms of air frying, I find myself reflecting on how this modern technique stands up against the time-honored tradition of frying.

Traditional frying involves submerging food in hot oil, which crisps the exterior while ideally keeping the interior moist. This method has graced us with countless gastronomic pleasures, from crispy calamari to tender arancini. However, it comes with its caveats—namely, the high amounts of oil required, which can lead to increased caloric intake and potentially harmful effects from consuming too much fried food.

Enter air frying, a beacon of modern culinary technology that promises to mimic the results of traditional frying with a fraction of the oil. This is achieved through a rapidly circulating hot air that cooks the food evenly and produces a crispy texture akin to deep frying. The reduction in oil not only lowers the calorie content but also diminishes the risk of issues associated with high-fat diets, such as heart disease and high cholesterol.

The contrast does not end with health benefits. In terms of practicality, air frying offers a cleaner, safer kitchen experience. Gone are the days of dodging splattering oil and facing the tedious aftermath of cleaning greasy pots and surrounding surfaces. An air fryer contains the heat and any minimal mess within its compact design, making it a friendly companion for both seasoned chefs and culinary novices.

Moreover, air frying distributes heat more evenly than many traditional methods, reducing instances of accidentally burnt offerings that even the most vigilant chef can fall prey to when juggling multiple pans on a busy stove. This precision allows for consistency in cooking, giving you perfect results with every use.

As we stand at the crossroads of culinary tradition and innovation, I find that air frying does not diminish the art of cooking but rather expands it. It provides a new canvas on which we can express our love for food, drawing from the best of both worlds—embracing the new without losing the essence of the old.

So, while my heart will always cherish the traditional ways, my adventurous spirit cannot help but be excited by the possibilities that air frying brings to our kitchens. Let us continue to fry, roast, and bake, but with an eye towards a healthier future and a nod to the conveniences of modern living.

Choosing the Right Air Fryer: Model Comparisons

In the bustling markets of Genoa, where I spent many years honing my culinary skills, choosing the right ingredients was paramount to the success of any dish. Similarly, selecting the right air fryer can be just as crucial for your kitchen adventures. As this wonderful appliance grows in popularity, the variety of models available can be as varied as the types of pasta in my beloved Italy.

First, let us consider the size. Air fryers range from compact models suitable for individuals or couples to larger units that can accommodate meals for a whole family. For those who entertain often or have a large family, a model with a greater capacity will prove indispensable. On the other hand, a smaller unit might be perfect for those with limited counter space or who typically cook for one or two.

Next, we look at functionality. While all air fryers offer the basic function of frying with less oil, some models come equipped with additional features such as grilling, baking, and roasting capabilities. Some even have preset functions for specific foods, ensuring perfect results every time. For the adventurous cook who likes to experiment with different cooking methods, a multi-functional air fryer could be a treasure trove of culinary potential.

Control settings also vary. Some air fryers keep it simple with manual dials, while others boast digital displays with timers and precise temperature controls. For those who appreciate the ability to set it and forget it, a digital model offers convenience and accuracy. However, for others, the tactile feedback of turning a dial might echo the familiar comfort of traditional cooking methods.

The ease of cleaning is another consideration. Look for air fryers with non-stick, dishwasher-safe baskets and trays to make cleanup a breeze. After all, a tool that simplifies cooking should not complicate your cleanup.

Lastly, consider the aesthetic appeal. As someone who values the beauty of a well-laid table, I understand that the appearance of your appliances matters, too. Air fryers come in a range of designs, from sleek and modern to retro, fitting beautifully into the decor of any kitchen.

Choosing the right air fryer is much like choosing the best olive oil—it all comes down to your personal needs and tastes. Whether you prioritize capacity, versatility, control, ease of maintenance, or style, there is an air fryer out there that is the perfect complement to your culinary style.

In this era of rapid technological advancement, even a traditional chef like myself finds joy in the fusion of old and new. Embrace these modern marvels, and let them help you craft dishes that bring joy to the table and health to your life.

Safety Tips and Best Practices for Using an Air Fryer

As with any culinary endeavor, safety in the kitchen is paramount. Whether you are a novice cook or an experienced chef like myself, understanding how to safely operate your appliances ensures not only the success of your dishes but also the well-being of everyone who gathers at your table. Here are some key safety tips and best practices for using your air fryer, shared with the care and attention to detail that I apply in my own kitchen in Genoa.

Read the Manual

Before you begin, familiarize yourself with your air fryer. Each model comes with its own set of instructions and recommendations. Taking the time to read the manual might not be as delightful as savoring a well-aged Pecorino, but it is just as essential. Understanding your appliance's specific capabilities and limitations ensures you use it correctly and safely.

Keep It Clear

Always ensure that the air intake and exhaust vents are clear. Air fryers work by circulating hot air, and blocking these vents can cause the unit to overheat, compromising its functionality and safety. Think of it as needing a clear chimney for a perfect wood-fired pizza; without this, the results could be disastrous.

Use Appropriate Cookware

If you are using additional pans or trays in your air fryer, make sure they are compatible with it. Just as you wouldn't use a delicate fish spatula to flip a hefty Florentine steak, you should ensure that your cookware is suitable for the environment of an air fryer.

Don't Overload

To achieve that perfectly crisp finish, do not overcrowd the basket. Air needs to circulate around the food for even cooking. It's akin to not overcrowding the pan when sautéing vegetables — give them space to breathe, and they will reward you with a delightful texture.

Use Oils Sparingly

While air fryers require less oil than traditional frying methods, using a little oil can help achieve an even golden color on your food. Opt for an oil sprayer or brush a light coating of oil onto your food. Choose oils with a higher smoke point to avoid any acrid smoke that can spoil the flavor of your lovingly prepared dishes.

Handle With Care

The basket and the contents will be very hot after cooking. Always handle with oven mitts or a sturdy kitchen towel. Ensure you also use caution when removing food as the hot oil can cause burns if not handled properly.

Keep It Clean

Regular cleaning prevents build-up of food and grease, which can be a fire hazard. A clean air fryer not only operates more efficiently but also ensures that your food tastes as intended, without the ghost of meals past lingering on the palate.

Stay Present

Finally, as with any cooking method, it is important to stay attentive. While air fryers are designed to be set and forget, the aroma of cooking food should be enjoyed but also monitored. This will prevent burning and ensure your dishes turn out as delicious as the recipes intend.

In embracing these safety tips and best practices, you will find that using an air fryer can be a joyful and rewarding addition to your culinary repertoire. Let us proceed with caution, care, and creativity, infusing every meal with the essence of both safety and flavor.

Mediterranean Air Frying: Tradition Meets Innovation

In the sun-kissed regions of the Mediterranean, where the air is seasoned with sea salt and history, the culinary traditions are as rich and deep as the blue waters themselves. As a chef who has spent a lifetime celebrating these flavors, from the bustling markets of Milan to the serene coasts of Liguria, the introduction of air frying technology presented a delightful paradox: How do we marry the age-old culinary customs with this newfangled cooking method?

The Mediterranean diet, revered for its health benefits and emphasis on fresh vegetables, fruits, grains, and healthy fats like olive oil, aligns beautifully with the principles of air frying. This innovative cooking method allows us to honor the nutritional integrity of these ingredients while embracing the convenience and health benefits of modern technology.

Embracing Less Oil

Traditional Mediterranean cooking often involves liberal use of olive oil, which, while healthy, can be heavy. Air frying dramatically reduces the need for oil, allowing the natural flavors and textures of the food to shine through. Imagine crispy, golden eggplants, zucchinis, or falafel balls, cooked with just a spritz of oil—each bite is a testament to both tradition and innovation.

Preserving Natural Flavors

The genius of air frying lies in its ability to encapsulate the essence of the food. It intensifies flavors without overshadowing them, much like how a simple drizzle of lemon enhances a fresh piece of fish caught off the Amalfi coast. Air frying can achieve similar effects, highlighting the natural taste of ingredients without the heaviness of traditional frying.

Healthier Versions of Classic Dishes

Consider the beloved dishes such as Moussaka, typically laden with oil through the frying of its eggplant. The air fryer offers a way to recreate this dish with far less oil, maintaining the delightful textures and layers of flavor that define it, but with a lighter, healthier profile that suits modern dietary preferences.

Innovative Combinations

The air fryer invites experimentation, encouraging us to combine traditional herbs and spices with less conventional ingredients for new, exciting dishes. For example, mixing grains like farro or barley with seasoned vegetables, all crisped to perfection in the air fryer, creates a delightful fusion that respects dietary traditions while offering a modern twist.

Sustainable Cooking

The efficiency of air fryers aligns with the Mediterranean emphasis on sustainability. Using less energy than conventional ovens and producing less waste, air fryers reflect our growing awareness of the need to preserve our environment—much like the Mediterranean culture's respect for its lush landscapes and bountiful seas.

As we navigate this new era of culinary arts, let us carry forward the legacy of Mediterranean cooking not just as a diet, but as a lifestyle—one that values health, flavor, and the joy of sharing meals with loved ones. With each dish that comes out of the air fryer, we celebrate not just the ease and health benefits it offers, but the rich, cultural tapestry that has woven the Mediterranean culinary identity through the centuries.

Through the pages of this book, I invite you to explore how air frying can complement the Mediterranean way—embracing the old while welcoming the new, and always, always, cooking from the heart.

Chapter 1. Breakfasts

Buongiorno, my dear friends and fellow food enthusiasts! As a retired Italian chef who has embraced the joy of cooking with an air fryer, I've discovered the wonders it can do from dawn till dusk. But, what's a day without a delightful start? In this special chapter, I invite you to bring a touch of the Mediterranean sunrise into your kitchens with hearty, wholesome breakfasts prepared in your trusty air fryer.

The Mediterranean morning is a celebration of fresh flavors and simple pleasures. Here, breakfast isn't just the first meal; it's the start of a daily culinary adventure. Inspired by the vibrant mornings of my youth and my travels across the sunny coasts of Italy and Greece, I've crafted these recipes to blend tradition with convenience.

From the crispy edges of a frittata bursting with garden vegetables to the warm, comforting spices of shakshuka, each recipe is designed to minimize your time in the kitchen while maximizing joy at your table. These dishes are not just nutritious, being layered with the goodness of the Mediterranean diet, but also quick to prepare, thanks to our modern kitchen marvel—the air fryer.

So, set your table under the morning sky, or just by a sunny window, and prepare to indulge in a breakfast that's as easy to make as it is delicious to eat. Here's to starting your day with a taste of the Mediterranean—may it bring you as much joy as a morning by the sea. *Buon appetito!*

Ingredients

- ⬥ 4 large ripe tomatoes, sliced 1/2 inch thick
- ⬥ 2 tablespoons olive oil
- ⬥ 1 teaspoon sea salt
- ⬥ 1/2 teaspoon freshly ground black pepper
- ⬥ 1 teaspoon dried oregano
- ⬥ 1 teaspoon dried basil
- ⬥ 1/2 teaspoon garlic powder
- ⬥ 2 tablespoons grated Parmigiano cheese
- ⬥ Fresh basil leaves, for garnish

Air-Fried Tomato Slices with Herbs

 10'   8'   4 👨‍🍳 Easy

For a brunch twist, top these delightful slices with a poached egg or crumbled feta cheese. Every bite will take you closer to the Mediterranean shores, right at the start of your day!

Directions

- ⬥ Prep the Tomatoes: Arrange tomato slices on a paper towel and pat dry to remove excess moisture.
- ⬥ Seasoning Mix: In a small bowl, combine olive oil, salt, pepper, oregano, basil, and garlic powder.
- ⬥ Apply Seasoning: Brush each tomato slice with the olive oil mixture on both sides.
- ⬥ Air Frying: Preheat the air fryer to 380°F. Place tomato slices in a single layer in the air fryer basket. Cook for 4 minutes, then flip and sprinkle with Parmigiano. Continue cooking for another 4 minutes or until golden and crisp.
- ⬥ Garnish and Serve: Garnish with fresh basil leaves before serving.

Nutritional values per serving - Calories: 90 Fat: 7 g Sodium: 300 mg Carbohydrates: 6 g Protein: 2 g

Ingredients

- 1 cup cooked and crumbled chorizo
- 4 large eggs, beaten
- 1/2 cup shredded cheddar cheese
- 1/4 cup diced bell peppers
- 1/4 cup diced onions
- 1/4 teaspoon salt
- 1/4 teaspoon black pepper
- 1 tablespoon olive oil
- 8 empanada discs (store-bought or homemade)
- Olive oil spray

Breakfast Empanadas

 20' 8' ✂ 4 👨‍🍳 Easy

Bringing a little bit of Latin flair to your morning has never been easier! Empanadas are a fantastic way to incorporate variety into your breakfast routine. If chorizo isn't your favorite, you can easily substitute it with cooked bacon, ham, or even sautéed mushrooms for a vegetarian twist. Remember, the key to perfect empanadas is not overfilling them, so they seal nicely and don't burst during cooking.

Directions

- Sauté Vegetables: In a skillet, heat olive oil over medium heat. Add onions and bell peppers, sautéing until soft, about 3-4 minutes.
- Cook Eggs: Add the beaten eggs to the skillet with vegetables, stirring until they begin to set. Mix in the cooked chorizo. Season with salt and pepper. Remove from heat and let cool slightly before stirring in the cheddar cheese.
- Fill Empanadas: Place the empanada discs on a flat surface. Spoon the egg and chorizo mixture onto one half of each disc, being careful not to overfill. Fold the discs over to form a half-moon shape. Use a fork to crimp the edges and seal them.
- Air Fry: Preheat the air fryer to 350°F. Spray the empanadas lightly with olive oil spray. Place them in the air fryer basket, ensuring they are not touching. Cook for 8 minutes or until golden and crispy.
- Serve: Allow the empanadas to cool slightly before serving. They can be served with a side of salsa or sour cream for dipping.

Nutritional values per serving - Calories: 350 Fat: 22 g Sodium: 700 mg Carbohydrates: 18 g Protein: 22 g

Fig and Ricotta Toast

 10' 5' 4 Easy

Combining the sweetness of figs with the creamy texture of ricotta on a crisp toast makes a simple yet splendid start to your day. For a little twist, try drizzling a bit of balsamic reduction over the top for a sweet and tangy finish. It's these little touches that bring a breakfast from good to great.

Ingredients

- 4 slices of whole-grain bread
- 1 cup fresh ricotta cheese
- 4 fresh figs, sliced
- 1 tablespoon honey
- 1/4 teaspoon ground cinnamon
- 2 tablespoons chopped walnuts (optional)
- Fresh basil leaves for garnish

Directions

- Prep the Toast: Place the bread slices in the air fryer basket. Air fry at 360°F for about 3-4 minutes or until they are lightly toasted.
- Assemble: Spread each slice of toasted bread with a generous layer of ricotta cheese. Top with sliced figs, a drizzle of honey, a sprinkle of cinnamon, and chopped walnuts if using.
- Serve: Garnish with fresh basil leaves before serving.

Nutritional values per serving - Calories: 250 Fat: 9 g Sodium: 180 mg Carbohydrates: 34 g Protein: 10 g

Halloumi and Vegetable Skewers

 15' 10' 4 🍳 Easy

Nothing celebrates the garden's bounty like these colorful skewers. A tip for an even more delightful flavor: marinade the vegetables in olive oil, lemon juice, and herbs for an hour before threading to deepen the flavors.

Ingredients

- 1 block (9 oz) halloumi cheese, cut into 16 cubes
- 1 large red bell pepper, cut into 16 pieces
- 1 large green bell pepper, cut into 16 pieces
- 1 zucchini, sliced into 16 rounds
- 1 red onion, cut into chunks
- 2 tablespoons olive oil
- 1 teaspoon smoked paprika
- 1/2 teaspoon ground cumin
- Fresh herbs (such as parsley or cilantro) for garnish
- Optional: a pinch of sumac for extra tang

Directions

- Preheat Air Fryer: Preheat your air fryer to 400°F.
- Prepare Skewers: Thread halloumi, bell peppers, zucchini, and onion alternately onto skewers.
- Season: Brush the skewers with olive oil and sprinkle evenly with smoked paprika and cumin.
- Air Fry: Place skewers in the air fryer basket. Cook for 10 minutes, turning halfway through, until the vegetables are tender and the halloumi is golden brown.
- Garnish: Sprinkle with fresh herbs and a pinch of sumac before serving.

Nutritional values per serving - Calories: 290 Fat: 22 g Sodium: 680 mg Carbohydrates: 10 g Protein: 14 g

Ingredients

- 6 large eggs
- 1/4 cup milk
- 1/2 cup diced red bell pepper
- 1/2 cup chopped zucchini
- 1/4 cup chopped red onion
- 1/4 cup crumbled feta cheese
- 2 tablespoons chopped fresh basil
- 1 teaspoon dried oregano
- Salt and pepper to taste
- 1 tablespoon olive oil
- Additional herbs or spices (optional): paprika or sumac

Mediterranean Vegetable Frittata

 10' 20' 4 Easy

A frittata is like a blank canvas for any chef, inviting you to paint with the vibrant colors and flavors of the Mediterranean. To make this dish even more special, try adding a sprinkle of turmeric before cooking; it'll bring a beautiful golden color and a healthy boost to your morning meal.

Directions

- Prepare Vegetables: In a mixing bowl, combine bell pepper, zucchini, and onion with olive oil, salt, and pepper.
- Cook Vegetables: Preheat the air fryer to 360°F. Place the vegetable mixture in the air fryer basket and cook for 10 minutes, stirring halfway through.
- Mix Eggs: While vegetables are cooking, whisk together eggs, milk, oregano, and additional spices (if using) in a bowl. Stir in the cooked vegetables, feta cheese, and fresh basil.
- Cook Frittata: Pour the egg and vegetable mixture into a greased air fryer-safe pan. Cook at 360°F for about 10 minutes or until the eggs are set and the top is lightly golden.

Nutritional values per serving - Calories: 200 Fat: 14 g Sodium: 320 mg Carbohydrates: 6 g Protein: 12 g

Ingredients

- 2 cups all-purpose flour
- 1 tablespoon baking powder
- 1 teaspoon salt
- 2 tablespoons fresh rosemary, chopped
- 1/2 cup pitted and chopped black olives
- 1 cup milk
- 1/4 cup olive oil
- 2 tablespoons honey
- Optional garnish: sea salt, additional rosemary, or sumac for a tangy twist

Olive and Rosemary Bread

 15' 25' 4 🎩 Easy

This bread is a tribute to the rustic, hearty flavors of the Mediterranean countryside. For a variation, try adding a handful of grated Parmigiano for a salty, umami twist that beautifully complements the olives and rosemary.

Directions

- Mix Dry Ingredients: In a large bowl, combine flour, baking powder, salt, and chopped rosemary.
- Add Olives: Stir in the chopped olives to distribute evenly.
- Combine Wet Ingredients: In another bowl, whisk together milk, olive oil, and honey.
- Make Dough: Pour wet ingredients into the dry mixture and stir until just combined.
- Prepare for Air Frying: Transfer the dough into a greased air fryer-safe baking pan. Optionally, sprinkle with a bit of sea salt, additional rosemary, or sumac on top.
- Air Fry: Cook in the air fryer at 350°F for about 25 minutes or until the bread is golden and a toothpick inserted into the center comes out clean.

Nutritional values per serving - Calories: 350 Fat: 14 g Sodium: 790 mg Carbohydrates: 49 g Protein: 6 g

Shakshuka Cups

 10' 15' 4 🎩 Easy

Inspired by the vibrant flavors of the Mediterranean, these Shakshuka Cups are a delightful twist on a classic dish. For a little extra zest, try adding a sprinkle of sumac or a dash of hot sauce before serving. This dish perfectly captures the essence of sharing a warm, loving meal, even in the brisk pace of morning routines.

Ingredients

- 4 large eggs
- 1 cup tomato sauce (Ch. 8, preferably spiced with cumin, paprika, and a pinch of chili flakes)
- 1 small onion, finely diced
- 1 red bell pepper, finely diced
- 2 cloves garlic, minced
- 1 teaspoon smoked paprika
- 1/2 teaspoon ground cumin
- Salt and pepper, to taste
- 4 tablespoons crumbled feta cheese
- 2 tablespoons chopped fresh parsley
- Olive oil spray

Directions

- Preheat Air Fryer: Set the air fryer to 375°F and allow it to preheat for a few minutes.
- Prepare Vegetables: In a bowl, combine the onion, bell pepper, garlic, smoked paprika, and cumin. Toss with a little olive oil, salt, and pepper.
- Assemble Cups: Lightly grease 4 silicone muffin cups with olive oil spray. Spoon a layer of the vegetable mixture into each cup, followed by a generous tablespoon of tomato sauce.
- Add Eggs: Crack an egg into each cup, being careful not to break the yolks. Top each egg with a sprinkle of salt and pepper.
- Air Fry: Place the muffin cups in the air fryer basket. Cook for about 10-15 minutes, or until the egg whites are set but yolks are still runny.
- Final Touch: Sprinkle crumbled feta cheese and chopped parsley over each shakshuka cup just before serving.

Nutritional values per serving - Calories: 180 Fat: 12 g Sodium: 320 mg Carbohydrates: 10 g Protein: 9 g

Spanakopita Bites

 20'   8'   4*   Easy

* serves 12 bites

Spanakopita bites are a crisp and delightful treat, perfect for a quick breakfast or a snack. The fusion of dill and lemon zest not only brings a burst of freshness but also compliments the tangy feta beautifully. If you enjoy a bit more heat, a small pinch of red pepper flakes to the filling can add a lovely warmth.

Ingredients

- 4 sheets of phyllo dough, thawed
- 1 cup cooked spinach, drained and chopped
- 1/2 cup feta cheese, crumbled
- 1/4 cup ricotta cheese
- 1 small onion, finely chopped
- 2 cloves garlic, minced
- 1 tablespoon fresh dill, chopped
- 1 teaspoon fresh oregano, chopped
- Zest of one lemon
- Salt and pepper, to taste
- Olive oil spray

Directions

- Preheat Air Fryer: Preheat the air fryer to 350°F.
- Prepare Filling: In a mixing bowl, combine spinach, feta, ricotta, onion, garlic, dill, oregano, lemon zest, salt, and pepper. Mix well to incorporate all flavors.
- Prepare Phyllo: Lay out a sheet of phyllo dough on a clean surface and lightly spray with olive oil. Stack another sheet on top, spray again, and cut into 6 equal squares.
- Assemble Bites: Place a spoonful of the spinach mixture in the center of each square. Fold the corners of the phyllo over the filling to form a small packet or bite.
- Air Fry: Place the spanakopita bites in the air fryer basket, ensuring they do not touch. Cook for 8 minutes or until golden and crispy.
- Serve: Allow to cool slightly before serving, as the filling can be very hot.

Nutritional values per serving - Calories: 150 Fat: 8 g Sodium: 400 mg Carbohydrates: 12 g Protein: 5 g

Ingredients

- 2 medium zucchinis, grated
- 1/2 cup feta cheese, crumbled
- 1/4 cup all-purpose flour
- 1/4 cup fresh parsley, finely chopped
- 2 green onions, finely chopped
- 1 large egg
- 1 clove garlic, minced
- 1/2 teaspoon ground cumin
- Salt and pepper to taste
- Olive oil spray

Zucchini and Feta Pancakes

 15'   10'   4*   Easy

* serves 8 pancakes

Adding a pinch of sumac to the zucchini mixture before cooking can introduce a delightful tangy note that pairs wonderfully with the salty feta. These pancakes are a marvelous way to start the day, bringing a touch of Mediterranean flair to your breakfast table.

Directions

- Prepare Zucchini: Place the grated zucchini in a colander, sprinkle with a little salt, and let sit for 10 minutes. Squeeze out as much liquid as possible.
- Mix Ingredients: In a large bowl, combine the drained zucchini, crumbled feta, flour, parsley, green onions, egg, garlic, cumin, salt, and pepper. Stir until well mixed.
- Form Pancakes: Shape the mixture into 8 small patties.
- Preheat Air Fryer: Preheat the air fryer to 360°F.
- Cook Pancakes: Place the zucchini patties in the air fryer basket, spray lightly with olive oil, and cook for 10 minutes, flipping halfway through, until golden and crispy.
- Serve: Serve hot, garnished with a sprinkle of fresh herbs or a dollop of Greek yogurt.

Nutritional values per serving - Calories: 120 Fat: 6 g Sodium: 200 mg Carbohydrates: 10 g Protein: 6 g

Chapter 2. Appetizers and Snacks

Ah, the Mediterranean appetizer—where each meal begins with a burst of flavor, promising more delights to come. In the warm kitchens of my youth in Milan, with comforting aromas of garlic and olive oil, appetizers were more than a meal's prelude; they were a celebration of spirit and flavor, showcasing the region's bountiful produce and vibrant culture.

Now, with the modern marvel of the air fryer, I find myself reinvigorating these traditional starters with both convenience and health in mind. The air fryer lets us indulge in the rich tapestry of Mediterranean flavors—succulent olives, creamy cheeses, crisp breads, and fresh vegetables—with a lighter touch suited for today's health-conscious world.

Imagine crispy falafel balls, lightly golden yet full of flavor, or artichoke hearts tenderly infused with herbs, using the air fryer to bring a delightful twist to these classic dishes. These recipes embody the Mediterranean diet—nutrient-rich, colorful, simple, and unpretentious.

Moreover, the air fryer simplifies cooking, making it accessible even on busy days. Whether hosting a gathering or seeking a quick, nutritious snack, these recipes make it easy to bring the joy and health of Mediterranean cooking into your home with ease and flair.

Let's embark on this culinary journey with olive branches and air fryers in hand, exploring a world where tradition meets innovation at every meal. Here's to cooking that warms the soul and nourishes the body—Mediterranean appetizers and snacks, reimagined for a new era.

Air-Fried Artichoke Hearts

 10'   12'   4   Easy

Did you know that artichokes are not only delicious but also packed with antioxidants? These delightful thistles have been a staple in Mediterranean diets for centuries. For a smoky twist, add a pinch of smoked paprika before cooking, which enhances the natural nuttiness of the artichokes. Remember, the secret to perfect air-fried artichokes is in ensuring they are well-dried and seasoned before they dance in the hot air of your fryer.

Ingredients

- 2 cans (14 oz each) of artichoke hearts, drained and halved
- 1 tablespoon olive oil
- 1 teaspoon garlic powder
- 1/2 teaspoon dried basil
- Salt and pepper to taste
- 1/4 cup grated Parmigiano cheese
- 1 tablespoon chopped fresh parsley for garnish

Directions

- Dry Artichokes: Pat the artichoke hearts dry with paper towels to remove excess moisture. This step is crucial for achieving a crispy texture.
- Season Artichokes: In a bowl, toss the artichoke hearts with olive oil, garlic powder, dried basil, salt, and pepper until evenly coated.
- Arrange for Cooking: Arrange the artichoke hearts in a single layer in the air fryer basket, ensuring they do not overlap. Sprinkle grated Parmigiano cheese over the top.
- Air Fry: Cook in the air fryer at 380°F for about 12 minutes, or until golden and crispy. Shake the basket halfway through to ensure even cooking.
- Serve: Serve hot, garnished with chopped fresh parsley.

Nutritional values per serving - Calories: 90 Fat: 5 g Sodium: 300 mg Carbohydrates: 8 g Protein: 4 g

Air-Fried Jalapeño Poppers

 15' 10' 4 Easy

To give these poppers a delightful twist, try adding a pinch of ground cumin to the cheese mixture for an earthy depth, or drizzle the finished poppers with a touch of honey for a sweet contrast to the spicy jalapeño. Remember, the beauty of cooking lies in making each dish your own!

Ingredients

- 12 jalapeño peppers, halved lengthwise and seeds removed
- 1 cup cream cheese, softened
- 1/2 cup shredded cheddar cheese
- 1/4 cup finely chopped cilantro
- 1 teaspoon smoked paprika
- 1/2 teaspoon garlic powder
- Salt and pepper to taste
- 1/2 cup panko breadcrumbs
- Olive oil spray

Directions

- Prepare Filling: In a mixing bowl, combine the cream cheese, cheddar cheese, cilantro, smoked paprika, garlic powder, salt, and pepper. Mix well until the filling is smooth and evenly seasoned.
- Fill Jalapeños: Spoon the cheese mixture into each jalapeño half, filling them generously.
- Breadcrumb Coating: Gently press the filled side of each jalapeño into the panko breadcrumbs to coat the top.
- Arrange for Air Frying: Arrange the jalapeño poppers in a single layer in the air fryer basket, ensuring they do not touch to allow air to circulate freely. Lightly spray the tops with olive oil.
- Air Fry: Cook in the air fryer at 370°F for about 10 minutes, or until the poppers are golden and crispy.
- Serve: Serve warm as a delightful starter or a spirited snack.

Nutritional values per serving - Calories: 200 Fat: 15 g Sodium: 300 mg Carbohydrates: 9 g Protein: 6 g

Ingredients

- 1 cup large green olives, pitted
- 1/2 cup all-purpose flour
- 1 teaspoon smoked paprika
- 1/2 teaspoon dried oregano
- 1 large egg, beaten
- 1 cup panko breadcrumbs
- 2 tablespoons grated Parmigiano cheese
- Olive oil spray

Air-Fried Olives

 10' 8' 4 Easy

Olives are not just for garnishing your favorite martini! This dish transforms them into a crunchy, irresistible snack. For a zesty twist, sprinkle the finished olives with a touch of lemon zest or chili flakes before serving, enhancing their Mediterranean roots with a bit of spice and zest.

Directions

- Mix Dry Ingredients: In a small bowl, mix the flour with smoked paprika and oregano.
- Prepare Dipping Stations: Place the beaten egg in a separate bowl, and mix the panko breadcrumbs with grated Parmigiano in another bowl.
- Prep Olives: Dry the olives with paper towels to ensure the coating sticks properly.
- Coat Olives: Dredge each olive first in the seasoned flour, then dip into the egg, and finally coat thoroughly in the panko-Parmigiano mixture.
- Arrange in Air Fryer: Arrange the breaded olives in a single layer in the air fryer basket, ensuring they are not touching to allow for even cooking. Spray lightly with olive oil.
- Air Fry: Cook in the air fryer at 390°F for about 8 minutes, or until golden and crispy, shaking the basket halfway through.
- Serve: Serve hot, perhaps with a side of marinara sauce for dipping (Ch. 8)

Nutritional values per serving - Calories: 180 Fat: 10 g Sodium: 400 mg Carbohydrates: 17 g Protein: 6 g

Ingredients

- 1 baguette, sliced into 1/2-inch rounds
- 2 tablespoons olive oil
- 2 ripe tomatoes, finely chopped
- 1 clove garlic, minced
- 1/4 cup basil leaves, chopped
- Salt and pepper to taste
- 1/4 cup shredded mozzarella cheese (optional)

BRUSCHETTA BITES

 10' 8' 4 👨‍🍳 Easy

Bruschetta is traditionally served as a fresh, vibrant antipasto in Italy. For a delightful twist, add a drizzle of balsamic glaze over the bruschetta bites before serving, enhancing the sweet freshness of the tomatoes with a rich, tangy accent. This dish pairs beautifully with a crisp white wine on a warm evening.

Directions

- **Prepare Baguettes:** Brush each baguette slice lightly with olive oil and arrange them in the air fryer basket in a single layer (you may need to work in batches).
- **First Air Fry:** Air fry at 360°F for 3 minutes until they are lightly toasted.
- **Mix Toppings:** In a small bowl, mix together the chopped tomatoes, garlic, basil, salt, and pepper.
- **Add Toppings:** Top each toasted baguette slice with a spoonful of the tomato mixture. If using, sprinkle a little mozzarella cheese on top.
- **Second Air Fry:** Return the topped slices to the air fryer and cook for another 5 minutes at 360°F, or until the cheese is melted and bubbly.
- **Serve:** Serve immediately..

Nutritional values per serving - Calories: 200 Fat: 9 g Sodium: 450 mg Carbohydrates: 25 g Protein: 6 g

CRISPY CHICKPEAS

 5' 15' 4 👨‍🍳 Easy

Crispy chickpeas are not only a delightful snack but also a versatile addition to salads and soups for an extra crunch. For a Mediterranean twist, sprinkle a dash of sumac before serving for its lemony zest, which pairs beautifully with the smokiness of paprika and the earthiness of cumin. Cooking from the heart means bringing layers of flavor and texture to even the simplest ingredients.

Ingredients

- 2 cans (15 oz each) chickpeas, rinsed, drained, and thoroughly dried
- 1 tablespoon olive oil
- 1 teaspoon smoked paprika
- 1/2 teaspoon ground cumin
- 1/4 teaspoon turmeric
- Salt and pepper to taste
- 2 tablespoons chopped fresh parsley for garnish

Directions

- **Dry Chickpeas:** Ensure the chickpeas are very dry after rinsing by patting them with paper towels. Removing moisture is key to getting them perfectly crispy.
- **Season Chickpeas:** In a bowl, toss the chickpeas with olive oil, smoked paprika, cumin, turmeric, salt, and pepper until evenly coated.
- **Arrange in Basket:** Spread the chickpeas in a single layer in the air fryer basket. Avoid overcrowding to ensure they cook evenly.
- **Air Fry:** Cook in the air fryer at 390°F for 15 minutes, shaking the basket every 5 minutes to promote even crisping.
- **Serve:** Once crispy and golden, transfer the chickpeas to a serving bowl and garnish with chopped parsley.

Nutritional values per serving - Calories: 210 Fat: 6 g Sodium: 400 mg Carbohydrates: 29 g Protein: 10 g

Feta and Spinach Rolls

 15'   10'   4   Easy

Phyllo dough can be a delightful canvas for your culinary creations, lending itself beautifully to both sweet and savory fillings. For a touch of zest, add a sprinkle of lemon zest to your spinach mixture before rolling. This not only brightens the flavor but also complements the salty feta wonderfully, bringing a hint of the Mediterranean breeze to every bite.

Nutritional values per serving - Calories: 270 Fat: 18 g Sodium: 580 mg Carbohydrates: 20 g Protein: 8 g

Ingredients

- 1 package (10 oz) frozen spinach, thawed and thoroughly drained
- 1 cup feta cheese, crumbled
- 1/4 cup fresh dill, finely chopped
- 2 green onions, finely chopped
- 1 teaspoon garlic powder
- Salt and pepper to taste
- 1 package filo dough, thawed
- 1/4 cup olive oil or melted butter for brushing

Directions

- Preheat Air Fryer: Preheat your air fryer to 360°F.
- Prepare Filling: In a bowl, mix the spinach, feta, dill, green onions, garlic powder, salt, and pepper until well combined.
- Prepare Phyllo: Lay out one sheet of phyllo dough on a clean surface (keep remaining dough covered with a damp cloth to prevent drying). Brush lightly with olive oil or melted butter.
- Add Filling: Place about 2 tablespoons of the spinach and feta mixture on the short end of the phyllo sheet, leaving a border at the edges.
- Roll and Seal: Roll up the phyllo, folding in the edges to seal the filling inside. Brush the outside lightly with more oil or butter.
- Cut and Arrange: Cut the roll into four equal pieces and place them in the air fryer basket, seam side down, ensuring they do not touch.
- Cook: Cook for 10 minutes, or until golden and crispy, turning halfway through if needed.
- Serve: Serve warm, garnished with a sprinkle of chopped dill or crumbled feta if desired.

Ingredients

- 1 lb. large shrimp, peeled and deveined
- 2 tablespoons olive oil
- 4 cloves garlic, minced
- Zest and juice of 1 lemon
- 1 teaspoon smoked paprika
- 1/2 teaspoon red chili flakes (optional)
- Salt and freshly ground black pepper to taste
- Fresh parsley, chopped (for garnish)
- Lemon wedges (for serving)

Nutritional values per serving - Calories: 180 Fat: 8 g Sodium: 400 mg Carbohydrates: 17 g Protein: 6 g

Garlic Lemon Shrimp

 10'   8'   4 Easy

Did you know shrimp can cook in the blink of an eye in the air fryer, retaining all their natural juiciness? For those who love a little extra kick, sprinkle a bit of freshly chopped cilantro instead of parsley before serving. It adds a fresh, vibrant twist that pairs beautifully with the zesty lemon and robust garlic flavors.

Directions

- Prepare Marinade: In a large bowl, combine olive oil, minced garlic, lemon zest, lemon juice, smoked paprika, chili flakes (optional), salt, and pepper. Mix well.
- Marinate Shrimp: Add shrimp to the marinade and stir to coat evenly. Allow to marinate for about 15 minutes at room temperature.
- Skewer Shrimp: Thread the marinated shrimp onto skewers, about 4-5 shrimp per skewer.
- Preheat Air Fryer: Set the air fryer to 400°F.
- Arrange Skewers: Place the shrimp skewers in the air fryer basket in a single layer without touching.
- Cook Shrimp: Cook for 8 minutes, turning halfway through, until shrimp are pink and fully cooked.
- Serve: Garnish with chopped parsley and serve with lemon wedges on the side.

Ingredients

- 4 large russet potatoes, washed and cut into wedges
- 2 tablespoons olive oil
- 4 cloves garlic, minced
- 1/2 cup grated Parmigiano cheese
- 1 teaspoon dried oregano
- 1/2 teaspoon smoked paprika
- Salt and freshly ground black pepper to taste
- Fresh parsley, finely chopped

GARLIC PARMESAN POTATO WEDGES

 10' 20' 4 Easy

Potatoes are a canvas for flavor, and nothing complements their earthy taste like the boldness of garlic and the richness of Parmigiano. For an extra layer of flavor, sprinkle a little crushed rosemary over the wedges before cooking. Not only does rosemary add a fragrant aroma, but it also brings a touch of Italian countryside to your dish.

Directions

- Preheat Air Fryer: Set the air fryer to 400°F.
- Season Potatoes: In a large bowl, toss potato wedges with olive oil, minced garlic, Parmigiano cheese, oregano, paprika, salt, and pepper until well coated.
- Arrange in Basket: Place the potato wedges in the air fryer basket in a single layer, working in batches if necessary.
- Cook Wedges: Cook for 20 minutes, shaking the basket halfway through, until the wedges are golden and crispy.
- Serve: Garnish the hot potato wedges with chopped parsley for a fresh touch.

Nutritional values per serving - Calories: 300 Fat: 10 g Sodium: 250 mg Carbohydrates: 45 g Protein: 8 g

HUMMUS CHIPS

 15' 10' 4 Easy

Ingredients

- 1 cup chickpea flour
- 1/4 teaspoon salt
- 1/4 teaspoon garlic powder
- 1/4 teaspoon smoked paprika
- 1/4 teaspoon cumin
- 1 tablespoon olive oil
- 1/2 cup water
- Fresh thyme or rosemary for garnish (optional)

Chickpeas have been a staple in Mediterranean cooking for centuries, not only for their delightful taste but also for their versatility. These hummus chips bring a modern twist to traditional flavors. For an extra kick, try adding a pinch of chili powder to the dough before baking. Enjoy these crispy delights with a fresh dip or on their own as a light, savory snack.

Directions

- Mix Dry Ingredients: In a mixing bowl, combine chickpea flour, salt, garlic powder, smoked paprika, and cumin. Stir well to evenly distribute the spices.
- Prepare Dough: Add olive oil and water to the dry ingredients. Mix until a smooth dough forms.
- Roll Out Dough: Divide the dough into two portions. Roll each portion between two pieces of parchment paper as thinly as possible.
- Shape Chips: Remove the top layer of parchment, cut the dough on the bottom layer into small triangles or your preferred chip shapes using a cutting board.
- Arrange in Air Fryer: Transfer the chips to the air fryer basket in a single layer. Work in batches if necessary.
- Cook Chips: Air fry at 350°F for about 10 minutes, or until crispy and slightly golden.
- Serve: Allow the chips to cool slightly, then serve garnished with fresh thyme or rosemary if desired.

Nutritional values per serving - Calories: 150 Fat: 5 g Sodium: 150 mg Carbohydrates: 20 g Protein: 6 g

Mini Calzones

 20'   8'   4*   Easy

* 2 calzones each

In Italy, calzones are a beloved treat, perfect for a grab-and-go meal. To add a twist, try substituting the pepperoni with sautéed vegetables or even prosciutto for a different flavor profile. Remember, the air fryer's ability to bake these mini delights to perfection while using less oil is a testament to how tradition can meet innovation on your plate.

Nutritional values per serving - Calories: 350 Fat: 15 g Sodium: 700 mg Carbohydrates: 35 g Protein: 18 g

Ingredients

- 1 lb. pizza dough (store-bought or homemade, Ch. 8)
- 1 cup ricotta cheese
- 1 cup mozzarella cheese, shredded
- 1/2 cup pepperoni slices, chopped
- 1/4 cup fresh basil, chopped
- 2 tablespoons tomato sauce (Ch. 8), plus extra for dipping
- 1 egg, beaten (for egg wash)
- Salt and pepper to taste
- Olive oil spray

Directions

- Preheat Air Fryer: Set the air fryer to 375°F.
- Prepare Dough: Divide the pizza dough into 8 pieces and roll each into a 5-inch circle on a floured surface.
- Mix Filling: Combine ricotta, mozzarella, chopped pepperoni, basil, and tomato sauce in a bowl. Season with salt and pepper.
- Assemble Calzones: Spoon the filling onto half of each dough circle, fold over to form a half-moon, and pinch edges to seal.
- Prepare for Cooking: Brush each calzone with beaten egg and spray lightly with olive oil.
- Air Fry: Place calzones in the basket in batches, ensuring they don't touch. Cook for 8 minutes until golden.
- Serve: Enjoy warm with extra tomato sauce for dipping.

Mozzarella Sticks

 10'   6'   4*   Easy

* 3 sticks each

Ah, the humble mozzarella stick, a delightful treat when made right. For an extra touch of Italy, sprinkle freshly grated Parmigiano and a pinch of chili flakes over the sticks right after cooking. The warmth from the sticks will melt the Parmigiano slightly, adding a deliciously rich flavor that complements the tangy marinara sauce beautifully.

Ingredients

- 12 mozzarella string cheese sticks
- 1/2 cup all-purpose flour
- 2 large eggs, beaten
- 1 cup panko breadcrumbs
- 1 teaspoon garlic powder
- 1 teaspoon dried oregano
- 1/2 teaspoon smoked paprika
- Salt and pepper to taste
- Marinara sauce, for dipping (Ch. 8)
- Fresh basil leaves, for garnish

Directions

- Freeze Mozzarella: Freeze mozzarella sticks for at least one hour or until solid.
- Preheat Air Fryer: Set the air fryer to 390°F.
- Prepare Coating Stations: Set up three dishes—one with seasoned flour, one with beaten eggs, and one with panko mixed with spices.
- Coat Mozzarella Sticks: Dip each stick in flour, then egg, then panko, pressing to adhere.
- Arrange in Air Fryer: Place in the basket in a single layer without touching. Work in batches if needed.
- Cook: Air fry for 6 minutes, turning halfway, until golden and crispy.
- Serve: Garnish with basil and serve with marinara sauce for dipping.

Nutritional values per serving - Calories: 280 Fat: 15 g Sodium: 460 mg Carbohydrates: 18 g Protein: 18 g

Ingredients

✧ 4 cups water
✧ 1 cup polenta (cornmeal)
✧ 1 teaspoon salt
✧ 1/2 teaspoon black pepper
✧ 1/4 cup grated Parmigiano cheese
✧ 1 tablespoon fresh rosemary, finely chopped
✧ Olive oil spray

POLENTA FRIES

 10'* 15'  4 Easy

* plus chilling time

Polenta, a staple of Northern Italy, is wonderfully versatile. For a smoky flavor, mix in a pinch of smoked paprika before chilling. It's fascinating that polenta once considered *peasant food*, has found its way into gourmet kitchens worldwide, celebrated for its simplicity and comfort.

Directions

✧ Cook Polenta: In a saucepan, bring water to a boil, add polenta and salt, reduce to low heat, and stir until thickened, about 5 minutes.
✧ Add Flavors: Remove from heat, stir in black pepper, Parmigiano, and rosemary.
✧ Set Polenta: Pour into a greased dish, spread evenly, and refrigerate until firm, about 2 hours.
✧ Cut Fries: Turn out set polenta onto a cutting board and cut into fries.
✧ Preheat Air Fryer: Set the air fryer to 400°F.
✧ Arrange Fries: Place fries in the air fryer basket in a single layer, spray with oil, and work in batches if needed.
✧ Air Fry: Cook for 15 minutes, turning halfway, until golden and crisp.
✧ Serve: Offer hot with your choice of dipping sauce, such as aioli or marinara (Ch. 8).

Nutritional values per serving - Calories: 210 Fat: 5 g Sodium: 590 mg Carbohydrates: 35 g Protein: 4 g

SPICY BUFFALO CAULIFLOWER BITES

 10' 20' 4 Easy

Ingredients

✧ 1 large head of cauliflower, cut into bite-sized florets
✧ 1 tablespoon olive oil
✧ 1/2 cup buffalo sauce (Ch. 8)
✧ 1 teaspoon garlic powder
✧ 1/2 teaspoon paprika
✧ Salt and pepper to taste
✧ Fresh parsley, chopped (for garnish)
✧ Blue cheese or ranch dressing (Ch. 8), for dipping

Buffalo sauce, traditionally used to spice up chicken wings, finds a new companion in cauliflower, proving that bold flavors can enhance even the humblest of vegetables. For those who enjoy a less fiery dish, try using a milder hot sauce or add a drizzle of honey to the buffalo sauce for a sweet counterbalance to the spice.

Directions

✧ Preheat Air Fryer: Set to 360°F.
✧ Season Cauliflower: In a bowl, toss cauliflower florets with olive oil, garlic powder, paprika, salt, and pepper.
✧ Arrange in Basket: Place seasoned cauliflower in the air fryer basket in a single layer, working in batches as needed.
✧ Initial Air Frying: Cook for 10 minutes, then shake or stir for even cooking.
✧ Add Buffalo Sauce: Drizzle buffalo sauce over the cauliflower, tossing to coat evenly.
✧ Final Air Frying: Return to air fryer and cook for another 10 minutes until tender and caramelized.
✧ Serve: Garnish with parsley and serve with blue cheese or ranch dressing.

Nutritional values per serving - Calories: 110 Fat: 7 g Sodium: 800 mg Carbohydrates: 10 g Protein: 3 g

STUFFED MINI BELL PEPPERS

 15' 10' 4* Easy

* 3 peppers each

Mini bell peppers are not only a colorful addition to any plate but also packed with flavor. For a Mediterranean twist, mix some chopped olives or sun-dried tomatoes into the filling before stuffing the peppers. This simple variation introduces a punch of flavor that perfectly complements the creamy texture of the ricotta and the sweet crunch of the bell peppers.

Ingredients

- ◇ 12 mini bell peppers, tops cut off and seeds removed
- ◇ 1 cup ricotta cheese
- ◇ 1/4 cup grated Parmigiano cheese
- ◇ 1/4 cup finely chopped fresh basil
- ◇ 1 clove garlic, minced
- ◇ Salt and pepper to taste
- ◇ 1/4 teaspoon crushed red pepper flakes (optional for heat)
- ◇ Olive oil spray

Directions

- ◇ Prepare Filling: In a mixing bowl, combine ricotta, Parmigiano, basil, garlic, salt, pepper, and red pepper flakes. Mix until smooth and creamy.
- ◇ Fill Peppers: Generously spoon the cheese mixture into each hollowed-out mini pepper.
- ◇ Arrange in Air Fryer: Place stuffed peppers in a single layer in the air fryer basket and spray lightly with olive oil.
- ◇ Cook: Air fry at 375°F for about 10 minutes, until peppers are tender and the filling is slightly golden.
- ◇ Serve: Enjoy warm as a starter or snack.

Nutritional values per serving - Calories: 150 Fat: 9 g Sodium: 200 mg Carbohydrates: 8 g Protein: 9 g

Ingredients

- ◇ 12 large button mushrooms, stems removed and finely chopped, caps intact
- ◇ 2 tablespoons olive oil
- ◇ 1/4 cup breadcrumbs
- ◇ 1/4 cup grated Parmigiano cheese
- ◇ 2 cloves garlic, minced
- ◇ 1 tablespoon chopped fresh parsley
- ◇ 1 tablespoon chopped fresh basil
- ◇ Salt and pepper to taste
- ◇ 1/4 teaspoon dried oregano

STUFFED MUSHROOMS WITH HERBS

 15' 10' 4* Easy

* 3 mushroom each

Mushrooms have a wonderful ability to absorb flavors, making them perfect for stuffing. For a little extra crunch and nutty flavor, add some finely chopped walnuts to the stuffing mixture before filling the mushrooms. Not only does this add texture, but walnuts are also rich in omega-3 fatty acids, enhancing the nutritional value of this delightful appetizer.

Directions

- ◇ Preheat Air Fryer: Set the air fryer to 360°F.
- ◇ Prepare Filling: In a bowl, combine chopped mushroom stems, breadcrumbs, Parmigiano, garlic, parsley, basil, salt, pepper, and oregano.
- ◇ Add Oil: Drizzle olive oil over the filling and mix until well combined.
- ◇ Stuff Mushrooms: Spoon the filling into each mushroom cap, packing it lightly.
- ◇ Arrange in Basket: Place stuffed mushrooms in a single layer in the air fryer basket, ensuring they do not touch.
- ◇ Cook: Air fry for 10 minutes, or until mushrooms are tender and tops are golden.

Nutritional values per serving - Calories: 150 Fat: 10 g Sodium: 200 mg Carbohydrates: 10 g Protein: 6 g

Ingredients

- 2 large sweet potatoes, peeled and cut into 1/4-inch thick fries
- 2 tablespoons olive oil
- 1 teaspoon paprika
- 1/2 teaspoon garlic powder
- Salt and freshly ground black pepper to taste
- Fresh parsley, finely chopped (for garnish)

Sweet Potato Fries

 10' 15' ✗ 4 👨‍🍳 Easy

Sweet potatoes are not only delicious but also rich in vitamins, fiber, and antioxidants. For an adventurous twist, sprinkle a pinch of cinnamon or cumin before cooking to enhance their natural sweetness with a warm, spicy note. This small touch can transform a simple side dish into a memorable part of your meal.

Directions

- Preheat Air Fryer: Set the air fryer to 380°F.
- Season Fries: In a large bowl, toss sweet potato fries with olive oil, paprika, garlic powder, salt, and pepper until well coated.
- Arrange in Basket: Place fries in a single layer in the air fryer basket, ensuring they do not overlap. Work in batches if needed.
- Cook Fries: Cook for 15 minutes, shaking the basket halfway through for even cooking.
- Serve: Transfer crispy fries to a serving dish, garnish with chopped parsley, and serve immediately.

Nutritional values per serving - Calories: 180 Fat: 7 g
Sodium: 150 mg Carbohydrates: 27 g Protein: 2 g

Zucchini Fritters

 15' 10' 4* Easy

* 2/3 fritters each

Ingredients

- 2 medium zucchinis, grated
- 1 teaspoon salt
- 1/2 cup all-purpose flour
- 1/4 cup grated Parmigiano cheese
- 2 cloves garlic, minced
- 1 large egg, beaten
- 1/2 teaspoon black pepper
- 2 tablespoons fresh basil, finely chopped
- Olive oil spray

Zucchini is a wonderfully versatile vegetable that beautifully absorbs flavors. For a Mediterranean twist, add a pinch of dried oregano or thyme to the batter. These herbs not only elevate the flavor but also bring a touch of Italian countryside to your table. Remember, cooking is about creativity and using what you have on hand to bring joy and health to your meals.

Directions

- Prepare Zucchini: Place grated zucchini in a colander, sprinkle with salt, and let sit for 10 minutes to draw out moisture. Squeeze out excess water using a clean dish towel or by pressing in the colander.
- Mix Ingredients: In a large bowl, combine drained zucchini, flour, Parmigiano, garlic, egg, black pepper, and basil. Stir until well combined and cohesive.
- Preheat Air Fryer: Set the air fryer to 390°F.
- Form Patties: Shape the zucchini mixture into small patties and set them on a plate.
- Arrange in Basket: Spray the air fryer basket with olive oil and place patties in the basket without touching. Spray the tops of the patties with olive oil.
- Cook Fritters: Cook for 10 minutes, flipping halfway, until fritters are golden and crispy.
- Serve: Garnish hot fritters with additional chopped basil or a dollop of yogurt or sour cream, if desired.

Nutritional values per serving - Calories: 150 Fat: 5 g
Sodium: 300 mg Carbohydrates: 20 g Protein: 6 g

Chapter 3. Main Courses

Ah, the Mediterranean table—a bountiful spread where each dish not only feeds the body but also nourishes the soul. As a retired chef with decades immersed in the flavors of Italy and its neighbors, I cherish the simplicity and freshness of Mediterranean cooking. From succulent meats and flavorful seafood to vibrant vegetables, this cuisine truly celebrates life.

Now, with the modern marvel of the air fryer, adapting these traditional main courses for today's health-conscious and busy cooks becomes a delightful challenge. The air fryer cooks food quickly with minimal oil, making it ideal for preparing wholesome, hearty meals that honor Mediterranean principles.

Using an air fryer, we can enjoy dishes like juicy lamb koftas or tender branzino, each infused with herbs and perfectly cooked, or golden, crispy eggplant Parmigiana, as satisfying as its traditionally fried counterpart but healthier.

In this section, I'll guide you through a variety of main courses from the shores of the Adriatic to the Greek islands. These recipes bring the essence of Mediterranean cooking into your home, proving that tradition and innovation can coexist beautifully on your dinner plate.

Let's embark on this flavorful adventure together, with olive oil in our hearts and air fryers at the ready. Here's to easy-to-prepare, delightful-to-savor main courses. *Buon appetito!*

Balsamic Glazed Chicken Breasts

Ingredients

- 4 boneless, skinless chicken breasts (6-8 oz each)
- 1 tablespoon olive oil
- Salt and freshly ground black pepper, to taste
- 1/2 cup balsamic vinegar
- 2 tablespoons honey
- 2 cloves garlic, minced
- 1 teaspoon dried Italian herbs or a mix of oregano, thyme, and rosemary
- Fresh basil leaves, for garnish

 10'   20'   4   Easy

Balsamic vinegar isn't just for salads! Its rich, complex sweetness enhances the depth of grilled or air-fried meats beautifully. For an added twist, sprinkle a few drops of aged balsamic vinegar over the cooked chicken before serving to introduce an extra layer of flavor that complements the honeyed glaze wonderfully.

Directions

- Preheat Air Fryer: Set the air fryer to 360°F.
- Prepare Chicken: Rub each chicken breast with olive oil and season generously with salt and pepper.
- Mix Glaze: In a small bowl, whisk together balsamic vinegar, honey, garlic, and dried herbs.
- Cook Chicken: Place the chicken breasts in the air fryer basket and cook for 10 minutes.
- Apply Glaze: Brush the balsamic mixture over the chicken breasts, then return them to the air fryer.
- Finish Cooking: Cook for an additional 10 minutes, or until the chicken is thoroughly cooked and the glaze has caramelized.
- Garnish and Serve: Garnish the chicken breasts with fresh basil leaves before serving.

Nutritional values per serving - Calories: 240 Fat: 7 g Sodium: 200 mg Carbohydrates: 15 g Protein: 26 g

Ingredients

- 1 lb. beef sirloin, cut into 1-inch cubes
- 1 red bell pepper, cut into 1-inch pieces
- 1 yellow bell pepper, cut into 1-inch pieces
- 1 zucchini, sliced into 1/2-inch rounds
- 1 red onion, cut into chunks
- 2 tablespoons olive oil
- 1 teaspoon paprika
- 1/2 teaspoon ground cumin
- Salt and freshly ground black pepper to taste
- 2 tablespoons fresh parsley, chopped
- Lemon wedges, for serving

BEEF AND VEGETABLE KEBABS

 20' 10' 4 Easy

Kebabs are a festive and versatile dish, ideal for gatherings or a family dinner. To bring a touch of Greek flair, marinate the beef in a mixture of olive oil, lemon juice, garlic, and oregano before threading on skewers. This not only tenderizes the meat but also infuses it with the vibrant flavors of the Mediterranean.

Directions

- Marinate Ingredients: In a large bowl, combine olive oil, paprika, cumin, salt, and black pepper. Add the beef cubes and vegetables, tossing to coat evenly.
- Skewer Beef and Vegetables: Thread the marinated beef and vegetables alternately onto skewers.
- Preheat Air Fryer: Set the air fryer to 400°F.
- Arrange Skewers: Place the skewers in the air fryer basket, spaced apart for even cooking.
- Cook: Cook for 10 minutes, turning halfway, until the beef reaches desired doneness and vegetables are tender and slightly charred.
- Garnish and Serve: Garnish with chopped parsley and serve with lemon wedges.

Nutritional values per serving - Calories: 250 Fat: 12 g Sodium: 75 mg Carbohydrates: 8 g Protein: 26 g

CHICKEN SOUVLAKI

 25'* 10' 4* Easy

* including marinating time

Ingredients

- 1 1/2 lbs. chicken breast, cut into 1-inch cubes
- 3 tablespoons olive oil
- Juice of 1 lemon
- 3 cloves garlic, minced
- 2 teaspoons dried oregano
- Salt and freshly ground black pepper to taste
- 1 red onion, cut into 1-inch pieces
- Fresh parsley, chopped (for garnish)
- Lemon wedges (for serving)

Souvlaki is more than just a dish; it's a Greek celebration on a skewer. To elevate this dish for a special occasion, try adding bell peppers and cherry tomatoes to the skewers before cooking. This not only adds vibrant color and variety but also enhances the flavor profile, making each bite a delightful exploration of Mediterranean tastes.

Directions

- Prepare Marinade: In a bowl, whisk together olive oil, lemon juice, minced garlic, oregano, salt, and pepper. Add the chicken cubes and toss to coat. Marinate in the refrigerator for 15 minutes to 2 hours.
- Preheat Air Fryer: Set the air fryer to 400°F.
- Assemble Skewers: Thread the marinated chicken and onion pieces alternately onto skewers.
- Arrange Skewers: Place the skewers in the air fryer basket, spaced apart for even cooking.
- Cook: Cook for 10 minutes, turning the skewers halfway through, until the chicken is golden brown and cooked through.
- Garnish and Serve: Garnish with chopped parsley and serve with lemon wedges.

Nutritional values per serving - Calories: 290 Fat: 16 g Sodium: 200 mg Carbohydrates: 4 g Protein: 34 g

Cod with Mediterranean Salsa

 15' 12' 4 Easy

Cod, a beloved fish across many cultures, pairs wonderfully with the robust flavors of the Mediterranean. For a twist, try grilling the lemon before squeezing it over the salsa—the charred citrus will add a smoky depth to the salsa that beautifully complements the mildness of the cod.

Ingredients

- 4 cod fillets (about 6 oz each)
- 2 tablespoons olive oil
- Salt and freshly ground black pepper to taste
- 1 cup cherry tomatoes, quartered
- 1/2 cup pitted Kalamata olives, chopped
- 1/4 cup red onion, finely chopped
- 1/4 cup fresh basil leaves, chopped
- 2 tablespoons capers, rinsed and drained
- Juice of 1 lemon
- 1 garlic clove, minced

Directions

- Preheat Air Fryer: Set the air fryer to 400°F.
- Prepare Cod: Brush cod fillets with olive oil and season with salt and pepper.
- Cook Cod: Place the cod in the air fryer basket and cook for 10-12 minutes, until the fish flakes easily with a fork.
- Make Salsa: While the cod cooks, combine cherry tomatoes, olives, red onion, basil, capers, lemon juice, garlic, and remaining olive oil in a bowl. Stir to mix.
- Assemble and Serve: Transfer cooked cod fillets to plates and top each with a generous portion of the Mediterranean salsa. Serve immediately.

Nutritional values per serving - Calories: 230 Fat: 12 g Sodium: 400 mg Carbohydrates: 6 g Protein: 23 g

Ingredients

- 2 medium eggplants, sliced into 1/2-inch thick rounds
- Salt, to draw out moisture from eggplant
- 2 eggs, beaten
- 1 cup breadcrumbs, mixed with 1 teaspoon Italian seasoning and 1/2 teaspoon garlic powder
- 1 cup marinara sauce (Ch. 8)
- 1 cup shredded mozzarella cheese
- 1/2 cup grated Parmigiano cheese
- Fresh basil leaves for garnish
- Olive oil spray

Nutritional values per serving - Calories: 350 Fat: 16 g Sodium: 700 mg Carbohydrates: 35 g Protein: 18 g

Eggplant Parmigiana

 15' 20' 4 Easy

Eggplant is like a sponge, absorbing flavors while cooking. To add a deeper flavor profile to your Eggplant Parmigiana, consider roasting a clove of garlic and mixing it into your marinara sauce before assembling. This simple twist will enrich the sauce with a mellow, sweet garlic flavor that complements the eggplant beautifully.

Directions

- Salt Eggplant: Sprinkle salt over the eggplant slices and let them sit for 10 minutes, then pat dry with paper towels.
- Bread Eggplant: Dip each eggplant slice into beaten eggs, then dredge in seasoned breadcrumbs, pressing to coat.
- Preheat Air Fryer: Set the air fryer to 375°F and spray the basket with olive oil.
- Arrange in Basket: Place breaded eggplant slices in a single layer in the basket; work in batches if necessary. Spray tops with olive oil.
- Initial Cooking: Cook for 10 minutes, flip each slice, and continue cooking for another 5 minutes until golden brown.
- Add Toppings: Top each slice with marinara sauce, mozzarella, and Parmigiano cheeses.
- Final Cooking: Return to the air fryer and cook for an additional 5 minutes, or until the cheese is bubbly and golden.
- Serve: Garnish with fresh basil leaves and serve hot.

Ingredients

- 8 large tomatoes, tops sliced off and insides hollowed out
- 1 cup cooked rice
- 1/2 cup crumbled feta cheese
- 1/4 cup finely chopped olives
- 1/4 cup finely chopped fresh parsley
- 1/4 cup finely chopped red onion
- 2 tablespoons olive oil
- 2 cloves garlic, minced
- Salt and freshly ground black pepper to taste
- 1 teaspoon dried oregano
- Fresh mint leaves, for garnish

Greek-Style Stuffed Tomatoes

 15'   10'   4*   Easy

* 2 tomatoes each

Tomatoes are not only a staple in Mediterranean cuisine but also a powerhouse of nutrition, rich in vitamins C and K, potassium, and folate. A fun fact about tomatoes—they were once believed to be poisonous in Europe until the late 18th century! Embracing them in dishes like this highlights how far culinary perceptions have evolved.

Directions

- Prepare Filling: In a bowl, combine cooked rice, feta cheese, olives, parsley, red onion, olive oil, garlic, salt, pepper, and oregano. Mix well.
- Stuff Tomatoes: Spoon the mixture into hollowed-out tomatoes, packing lightly.
- Preheat Air Fryer: Set the air fryer to 360°F.
- Arrange Tomatoes: Place the stuffed tomatoes in the air fryer basket; cook in batches if necessary.
- Cooking Time: Cook for 10 minutes, or until the tomatoes are heated through and slightly softened.
- Serve: Garnish with fresh mint leaves and serve warm.

Nutritional values per serving - Calories: 200 Fat: 10 g Sodium: 300 mg Carbohydrates: 24 g Protein: 6 g

Herb-Crusted Pork Tenderloin

 10'   20'   4   Easy

Ingredients

- 1 pork tenderloin (approximately 1 to 1.5 lbs.)
- 2 tablespoons olive oil
- 2 cloves garlic, minced
- 1 tablespoon fresh rosemary, finely chopped
- 1 tablespoon fresh thyme, finely chopped
- 1 tablespoon fresh sage, finely chopped
- Salt and freshly ground black pepper, to taste

Herbs are the heart and soul of Mediterranean cooking, turning simple ingredients into sensational meals. Did you know rosemary is not just flavorful but also packed with antioxidants and anti-inflammatory compounds? It's a delightful herb that enhances both the taste and the health benefits of your dishes.

Directions

- Prepare Pork: Pat the pork tenderloin dry with paper towels, rub with olive oil and minced garlic.
- Season: In a small bowl, mix rosemary, thyme, sage, salt, and pepper. Coat the pork evenly with this herb mixture.
- Preheat Air Fryer: Set to 400°F.
- Cook Pork: Place the pork in the air fryer basket and cook for 20 minutes, or until the internal temperature reaches 145°F.
- Rest: Remove pork from the air fryer and let rest for 5 minutes to retain juices.
- Serve: Slice and garnish with fresh herbs if desired.

Nutritional values per serving - Calories: 220 Fat: 12 g Sodium: 75 mg Carbohydrates: 1 g Protein: 24 g

Honey Garlic Glazed Chicken Wings

 10' 25' 4* Easy

* about 5 wings each

While honey and garlic might seem like a simple combination, they bring out the best in each other, offering a perfect balance of sweetness and pungency. This glaze not only enhances the wings but can also be brushed on grilled vegetables or other types of protein like shrimp or pork ribs for a delightful twist.

Ingredients

✧ 20 chicken wings, tips removed and cut at the joint
✧ 1/4 cup honey
✧ 3 tablespoons soy sauce
✧ 4 cloves garlic, minced
✧ 1 tablespoon olive oil
✧ 1/2 teaspoon ground black pepper
✧ 1/2 teaspoon paprika
✧ Fresh parsley, chopped (for garnish)

Directions

✧ Prepare Marinade: In a large bowl, whisk together honey, soy sauce, minced garlic, olive oil, black pepper, and paprika.
✧ Marinate Chicken: Add chicken wings to the marinade, toss to coat, and marinate for at least 10 minutes or refrigerate for one hour for deeper flavor.
✧ Preheat Air Fryer: Set to 380°F.
✧ Arrange Wings: Place marinated chicken wings in a single layer in the air fryer basket, working in batches if necessary.
✧ Cook: Fry for 25 minutes, turning wings halfway through until golden brown and crispy.
✧ Serve: Garnish with chopped parsley and serve hot.

Nutritional values per serving - Calories: 290 Fat: 18 g Sodium: 600 mg Carbohydrates: 11 g Protein: 24 g

Ingredients

✧ 4 Italian sausages (about 1 lb.)
✧ 2 bell peppers (one red, one yellow), sliced
✧ 1 large onion, sliced
✧ 2 tablespoons olive oil
✧ 1 teaspoon dried oregano
✧ Salt and freshly ground black pepper to taste
✧ Fresh basil leaves, for garnish

Italian Sausage and Peppers

 10' 20' 4 Easy

Italian sausages are versatile and packed with flavors from spices like fennel and paprika. For those looking to add a little heat, opt for spicy Italian sausage or add a sprinkle of crushed red pepper flakes to the vegetables before cooking. It's a simple way to heat up the dish and add an extra layer of flavor!

Directions

✧ Prepare Vegetables: In a large bowl, toss sliced bell peppers and onion with olive oil, oregano, salt, and pepper.
✧ Preheat Air Fryer: Set to 400°F.
✧ Arrange Sausages and Vegetables: Place sausages in the air fryer basket and surround with seasoned peppers and onions.
✧ First Cooking Phase: Cook for 10 minutes, then flip sausages and stir vegetables.
✧ Second Cooking Phase: Continue cooking for another 10 minutes or until sausages are browned and vegetables are tender and caramelized.
✧ Serve: Garnish with fresh basil leaves and serve hot.

Nutritional values per serving - Calories: 320 Fat: 24 g Sodium: 800 mg Carbohydrates: 10 g Protein: 14 g

Ingredients

- 1 lb. ground lamb
- 2 cloves garlic, minced
- 1 small onion, finely chopped
- 2 tablespoons fresh parsley, finely chopped
- 1 teaspoon ground cumin
- 1 teaspoon paprika
- 1/2 teaspoon ground coriander
- 1/4 teaspoon ground cinnamon
- Salt and freshly ground black pepper to taste
- Fresh mint leaves, for garnish

Lamb Kofta

 15'   10'   4*   Easy

* 2 koftas each

The beauty of koftas lies in their versatility. You can swap lamb for beef or chicken as a lighter alternative, and experiment with spices to find your favorite flavor profile. Try adding a touch of sumac for a tangy twist, which complements the richness of lamb beautifully and adds a burst of color to the dish.

Directions

- Mix Ingredients: In a large bowl, combine ground lamb, garlic, onion, parsley, cumin, paprika, coriander, cinnamon, salt, and pepper until well combined.
- Shape Koftas: Divide the mixture into eight parts and shape each around a skewer into a cylinder.
- Preheat Air Fryer: Set to 400°F.
- Arrange in Basket: Place lamb koftas in the air fryer basket, spaced apart for even cooking.
- Cook: Cook for 10 minutes, turning halfway, until koftas are browned and cooked through.
- Serve: Garnish with fresh mint leaves and serve hot.

Nutritional values per serving - Calories: 280 Fat: 22 g Sodium: 75 mg Carbohydrates: 2 g Protein: 19 g

Lemon Herb Chicken Thighs

 10'   25'   4   Easy

Ingredients

- 8 chicken thighs, bone-in and skin-on
- 2 tablespoons olive oil
- Juice of 1 lemon
- 2 cloves garlic, minced
- 1 tablespoon fresh rosemary, chopped
- 1 tablespoon fresh thyme, chopped
- Salt and freshly ground black pepper to taste
- Lemon slices and additional fresh herbs for garnish

Lemon and chicken are a match made in culinary heaven, but adding fresh herbs like rosemary and thyme elevates the simple combination to a dish full of aroma and flavor. For a slight twist, try grilling the lemon slices briefly in the air fryer before serving; this enhances their juiciness and adds a smoky, tangy flavor to the dish.

Directions

- Prepare Marinade: In a large bowl, mix olive oil, lemon juice, garlic, rosemary, thyme, salt, and pepper. Coat the chicken thighs evenly.
- Marinate Chicken: Refrigerate the chicken for at least 30 minutes to enhance flavors.
- Preheat Air Fryer: Set to 380°F.
- Cook Chicken: Place chicken thighs skin-side down in the air fryer basket; cook for 15 minutes.
- Flip and Finish Cooking: Turn chicken skin-side up and cook for another 10 minutes or until golden brown and internal temperature is 165°F.
- Garnish and Serve: Garnish with lemon slices and fresh herbs.

Nutritional values per serving - Calories: 310 Fat: 23 g Sodium: 220 mg Carbohydrates: 1 g Protein: 24 g

Mediterranean Stuffed Peppers

 15'   20'   4   Easy

Mediterranean cuisine is not only about flavors but also about colors and textures. Adding raisins to the stuffed peppers introduces a sweet contrast that complements the salty feta and briny olives beautifully. For those who enjoy a little extra spice, a sprinkle of crushed red pepper flakes can be added to the filling before cooking to warm up the dish with a bit of Mediterranean heat.

Ingredients

- 4 large bell peppers, tops cut off and seeds removed
- 1 cup cooked quinoa (Ch. 8)
- 1/2 cup crumbled feta cheese
- 1/2 cup chopped kalamata olives
- 1/4 cup diced red onion
- 1/4 cup chopped fresh parsley
- 1/4 cup raisins or dried currants
- 2 tablespoons olive oil
- 1 teaspoon dried oregano
- Salt and freshly ground black pepper to taste
- Fresh mint, for garnish

Directions

- Prepare Filling: In a bowl, combine cooked quinoa, feta cheese, kalamata olives, red onion, parsley, raisins, olive oil, oregano, salt, and pepper.
- Stuff Peppers: Fill each hollowed-out bell pepper with the quinoa mixture.
- Preheat Air Fryer: Set to 360°F.
- Cook Stuffed Peppers: Place in the air fryer basket and cook for 20 minutes, or until peppers are tender.
- Serve: Garnish with fresh mint leaves and serve hot.

Nutritional values per serving - Calories: 250 Fat: 15 g Sodium: 400 mg Carbohydrates: 23 g Protein: 8 g

Ingredients

- 8 chicken thighs, bone-in and skin-on
- 2 tablespoons olive oil
- 1 teaspoon ground cumin
- 1 teaspoon paprika
- 1/2 teaspoon ground turmeric
- 1/2 teaspoon ground coriander
- 1/4 teaspoon ground cinnamon
- Salt and freshly ground black pepper to taste
- 2 cloves garlic, minced
- Fresh cilantro, chopped for garnish
- Lemon wedges, for serving

Moroccan Spiced Chicken Thighs

 15'   20'   4  Easy

The blend of spices in this dish isn't just flavorful—it's also filled with health benefits. For instance, turmeric is renowned for its anti-inflammatory properties. To switch things up, consider adding a small pinch of saffron to the marinade for a luxurious touch and a richer color, enhancing the dish with both flavor and visual appeal.

Directions

- Prepare Marinade: In a large bowl, combine olive oil, cumin, paprika, turmeric, coriander, cinnamon, salt, pepper, and garlic.
- Marinate Chicken: Add chicken thighs and toss to coat evenly. Marinate for 30 minutes to 2 hours in the refrigerator.
- Preheat Air Fryer: Set to 380°F.
- Cook Chicken: Place thighs in the air fryer basket in a single layer and cook for 20 minutes, turning halfway.
- Serve: Garnish with chopped cilantro and accompany with lemon wedges.

Nutritional values per serving - Calories: 310 Fat: 23 g Sodium: 300 mg Carbohydrates: 2 g Protein: 24 g

Ingredients

- 4 salmon fillets (about 6 oz each)
- 1/2 cup prepared pesto (Ch. 8)
- 1/4 cup breadcrumbs
- 2 tablespoons grated Parmigiano cheese
- Olive oil spray
- Lemon wedges, for serving
- Fresh basil leaves, for garnish

Pesto-Crusted Salmon

 10' 12' ✗ 4 Easy

Salmon and pesto are a culinary duo that brings the lush gardens of Italy straight to your plate. For an extra touch of freshness, try making your own pesto with basil fresh from the garden, adding a more vibrant flavor to the fish. Also, adding a sprinkle of crushed pine nuts over the top before serving can introduce a delightful crunch that contrasts beautifully with the tender fish.

Directions

- Prepare Topping: In a small bowl, mix together the pesto, breadcrumbs, and Parmigiano cheese to create a coarse crumb mixture.
- Prepare Salmon: Pat the salmon fillets dry and place them skin-side down in a lightly oiled air fryer basket.
- Add Topping: Generously top each fillet with the pesto mixture, pressing to adhere.
- Preheat Air Fryer: Set to 375°F.
- Cook Salmon: Cook for 12 minutes, or until the topping is golden and salmon flakes easily.
- Serve: Garnish with fresh basil leaves and offer lemon wedges on the side.

Nutritional values per serving - Calories: 330 Fat: 23 g Sodium: 320 mg Carbohydrates: 4 g Protein: 23 g

Salmon with Dill and Lemon

 5' 12' 4 Easy

Ingredients

- 4 salmon fillets (about 6 oz each)
- 2 tablespoons olive oil
- 1 lemon, half juiced and half sliced
- 2 tablespoons fresh dill, finely chopped
- Salt and freshly ground black pepper, to taste
- Additional dill sprigs and lemon wedges, for garnish

Lemon and dill are not just flavorful—they're also powerhouses of nutrition. Dill is known for its digestive benefits, while lemon boosts the immune system with vitamin C. For an extra zest, grate some lemon zest over the salmon before serving to enhance the citrusy aroma and flavor, making the dish even more refreshing.

Directions

- Season Fillets: Drizzle each salmon fillet with olive oil and lemon juice, then season with salt and pepper. Sprinkle chopped dill evenly over the fillets.
- Preheat Air Fryer: Set the air fryer to 400°F.
- Prepare for Cooking: Place the salmon fillets in the air fryer basket, skin-side down, and top each with a slice of lemon.
- Cook Salmon: Cook for 12 minutes, or until the salmon is thoroughly cooked and flakes easily.
- Serve: Garnish with extra dill sprigs and provide lemon wedges on the side.

Nutritional values per serving - Calories: 280 Fat: 20 g Sodium: 75 mg Carbohydrates: 1 g Protein: 23 g

Shrimp and Vegetable Skewers

 15'   8'   4   Easy

* 2 skewers each

Shrimp cook quickly, making them a perfect candidate for a healthy, fast meal. The smokiness of paprika not only imparts a delightful flavor but also gives the illusion of grilling. To enhance the Mediterranean flair, consider a splash of lemon juice or a sprinkle of dried oregano before serving for that extra zing!

Ingredients

- 16 large shrimp, peeled and deveined
- 1 large zucchini, cut into 1/2-inch slices
- 1 red bell pepper, cut into 1-inch pieces
- 1 yellow bell pepper, cut into 1-inch pieces
- 1 red onion, cut into wedges
- 2 tablespoons olive oil
- 1 teaspoon smoked paprika
- 1/2 teaspoon garlic powder
- Salt and freshly ground black pepper, to taste
- Fresh parsley, chopped (for garnish)

Directions

- Prepare Marinade: In a large bowl, combine olive oil, smoked paprika, garlic powder, salt, and pepper.
- Coat Ingredients: Add the shrimp, zucchini, bell peppers, and onion to the bowl and toss to coat evenly with the marinade.
- Assemble Skewers: Thread the shrimp and vegetables alternately onto skewers.
- Preheat Air Fryer: Set the air fryer to 400°F.
- Cook Skewers: Place the skewers in the air fryer basket, ensuring they don't touch for even cooking. Cook for 8 minutes, turning halfway through.
- Serve: Garnish with chopped parsley and serve immediately.

Nutritional values per serving - Calories: 180 Fat: 10 g Sodium: 120 mg Carbohydrates: 8 g Protein: 12 g

Ingredients

- 4 chicken breasts (6-8 oz each)
- 1 cup fresh spinach, chopped
- 1/2 cup feta cheese, crumbled
- 2 tablespoons cream cheese, softened
- 1 clove garlic, minced
- 1 teaspoon dried oregano
- Salt and freshly ground black pepper, to taste
- 1 tablespoon olive oil
- Fresh dill, chopped (for garnish)

Spinach and Feta Stuffed Chicken Breasts

 20'   22'   4   Easy

Feta cheese not only adds a tangy kick to this dish but also provides a good amount of calcium. To make this dish even lighter, you can substitute cream cheese with Greek yogurt, adding a bit more protein and a creamy texture without the extra fat.

Directions

- Prepare Chicken: Make a pocket in each chicken breast by cutting a horizontal slit along one side, ensuring not to cut all the way through.
- Mix Filling: In a bowl, combine chopped spinach, feta cheese, cream cheese, minced garlic, oregano, salt, and pepper.
- Stuff Chicken: Fill each chicken breast with the spinach and feta mixture.
- Season Chicken: Brush the outside of the chicken breasts with olive oil and season lightly with salt and pepper.
- Preheat Air Fryer: Set the air fryer to 375°F.
- Cook Chicken: Place the stuffed chicken breasts in the air fryer basket, spaced apart for even cooking. Cook for 22 minutes.
- Serve: Garnish with chopped dill and serve hot.

Nutritional values per serving - Calories: 290 Fat: 15 g Sodium: 420 mg Carbohydrates: 3 g Protein: 31 g

Chapter 4. Side Dishes

In the sun-kissed realms of the Mediterranean, where the seas whisper to the bustling markets and cafes, the art of a meal extends beyond the main courses. The true spirit of Mediterranean culinary tradition shines in the side dishes—simple yet savory, they transform a meal into a vibrant symphony of flavors and textures, each telling its own story.

As a young boy in Milan and later as a chef in Genoa, I discovered that the secret to a memorable meal often lies in its sides. From the crispy, golden polenta of the north to the bright, zesty salads of the coast, each dish is a testament to the region's bounty.

In this chapter, using the air fryer, we dive into side dishes that enhance any meal with Mediterranean flair. We'll see how traditional ingredients like zucchini, eggplant, and tomatoes can become delightful accompaniments that stand proudly on their own. The air fryer's ability to crisp without excess oil allows us to reimagine these classics, making them lighter yet flavor-rich.

Crafted to bring ease and nutrition, these recipes are infused with herbs and spices synonymous with Mediterranean cuisine. From creamy risottos to tangy roasted vegetables, each dish carries the essence of the Mediterranean diet—simple, healthful, and delicious. Join me as we continue our culinary journey, turning simple ingredients into extraordinary experiences, and celebrating the colors, textures, and flavors that make Mediterranean sides a feast for the senses.

Air-Fried Greek Potatoes

 10' 20' 4 Easy

The key to perfect Greek potatoes lies in the simplicity of its seasoning. The addition of lemon wedges squeezed over the hot potatoes just before serving awakens the flavors and adds a refreshing zest. For those who love a bit of heat, a sprinkle of chili flakes before serving can make these potatoes even more delightful.

Ingredients

✧ 1.5 lbs. of baby potatoes, halved
✧ 2 tablespoons olive oil
✧ 1 teaspoon dried oregano
✧ 1/2 teaspoon garlic powder
✧ 1/2 teaspoon paprika
✧ Salt and freshly ground black pepper, to taste
✧ Fresh parsley, chopped (for garnish)
✧ Lemon wedges, for serving

Directions

✧ Season Potatoes: In a large bowl, toss the halved baby potatoes with olive oil, oregano, garlic powder, paprika, salt, and black pepper until evenly coated.
✧ Preheat Air Fryer: Preheat the air fryer to 400°F.
✧ Arrange in Basket: Arrange the potatoes in the air fryer basket in a single layer, ensuring they do not overlap for even cooking.
✧ Cook: Cook for 20 minutes, shaking the basket halfway through, until the potatoes are golden and crispy.
✧ Serve: Serve hot, garnished with chopped parsley and lemon wedges on the side.

Nutritional values per serving - Calories: 200 Fat: 7 g Sodium: 100 mg Carbohydrates: 31 g Protein: 3 g

Balsamic Roasted Brussels Sprouts

 10'   18'   4   🍳 Easy

The sweet and tangy flavor of balsamic vinegar enhances the natural nuttiness of Brussels sprouts, making this dish a delightful surprise. For a seasonal twist, try adding a handful of dried cranberries or roasted nuts in the last few minutes of cooking for extra texture and festive flair.

Ingredients

- ✧ 1 lb. Brussels sprouts, trimmed and halved
- ✧ 2 tablespoons olive oil
- ✧ 3 tablespoons balsamic vinegar
- ✧ 1 teaspoon honey
- ✧ Salt and freshly ground black pepper, to taste
- ✧ 2 tablespoons grated Parmigiano cheese (optional, for garnish)
- ✧ Fresh thyme leaves (for garnish)

Directions

- ✧ Mix Ingredients: In a large bowl, combine the Brussels sprouts with olive oil, balsamic vinegar, honey, salt, and pepper. Toss well to coat evenly.
- ✧ Preheat Air Fryer: Preheat the air fryer to 375°F.
- ✧ Arrange Sprouts: Spread the Brussels sprouts in an even layer in the air fryer basket, ensuring they do not overlap for uniform cooking.
- ✧ Cooking Time: Cook for 18 minutes, stirring halfway through, until the Brussels sprouts are tender on the inside and caramelized on the outside.
- ✧ Serve: Once cooked, transfer the Brussels sprouts to a serving dish. If desired, sprinkle with grated Parmigiano cheese and garnish with fresh thyme leaves before serving.

Nutritional values per serving - Calories: 130 Fat: 7 g Sodium: 75 mg Carbohydrates: 14 g Protein: 4 g

Ingredients

- ✧ 1 large head of broccoli, cut into florets
- ✧ 2 tablespoons olive oil
- ✧ 2 cloves garlic, minced
- ✧ 1/2 lemon, juiced and zest grated
- ✧ Salt and freshly ground black pepper, to taste
- ✧ Parmigiano cheese, freshly grated (for garnish)
- ✧ Red pepper flakes (optional, for garnish)

Broccoli with Lemon and Garlic

 10'   12'   4   🍳 Easy

Adding lemon zest before air frying not only imparts a zesty, bright flavor but also maximizes the aromatic oils, enhancing the dish's freshness. For those who enjoy a crunch, a sprinkle of toasted pine nuts or breadcrumbs tossed in during the last few minutes of cooking can add a delightful texture.

Directions

- ✧ Prepare Broccoli: In a large bowl, toss the broccoli florets with olive oil, minced garlic, lemon juice, lemon zest, salt, and black pepper until evenly coated.
- ✧ Preheat Air Fryer: Set the air fryer to 360°F.
- ✧ Arrange in Basket: Place the broccoli florets in the air fryer basket in a single layer to ensure they do not overlap for even cooking.
- ✧ Cooking Process: Cook for 12 minutes, shaking the basket halfway through, until the broccoli is tender and slightly crispy on the edges.
- ✧ Serve: Transfer the cooked broccoli to a serving dish and garnish with freshly grated Parmigiano cheese and a sprinkle of red pepper flakes if desired.

Nutritional values per serving - Calories: 110 Fat: 7 g Sodium: 80 mg Carbohydrates: 10 g Protein: 4 g

Ingredients

- ✧ 1 lb. Brussels sprouts, trimmed and halved
- ✧ 2 tablespoons olive oil
- ✧ 2 tablespoons capers, drained
- ✧ 1 clove garlic, minced
- ✧ Salt and freshly ground black pepper, to taste
- ✧ 1/2 lemon, juiced
- ✧ Parmigiano cheese, shaved (for garnish)

Brussels Sprouts with Capers

 10'   15'   4   Easy

Capers add a delightful burst of flavor, giving these Brussels sprouts a Mediterranean twist. They are not only packed with flavor but also rich in antioxidants. For a nutty variation, try tossing in a handful of pine nuts during the last few minutes of cooking for an added texture and rich flavor.

Directions

- ✧ Prepare Sprouts: In a bowl, toss the Brussels sprouts with olive oil, capers, minced garlic, salt, and pepper until well coated.
- ✧ Preheat Air Fryer: Preheat the air fryer to 375°F.
- ✧ Arrange in Basket: Arrange the Brussels sprouts in the air fryer basket in a single layer, ensuring they do not overlap for even cooking.
- ✧ Cooking Process: Cook for 15 minutes, shaking the basket halfway through, until the Brussels sprouts are crispy and golden.
- ✧ Finish and Serve: Transfer the cooked Brussels sprouts to a serving dish, and squeeze the lemon juice over them. Garnish with shaved Parmigiano cheese before serving.

Nutritional values per serving - Calories: 120 Fat: 7 g Sodium: 150 mg Carbohydrates: 10 g Protein: 4 g

Crispy Asparagus Spears

 5'   6'   4   Easy

Asparagus is not just a spring delight but a powerhouse of nutrients, including fiber, folate, and vitamins A, C, and K. For a playful twist, try drizzling with a bit of balsamic reduction after cooking, or for a crunch, top with slivered almonds before serving.

Ingredients

- ✧ 1 lb. fresh asparagus, trimmed
- ✧ 2 tablespoons olive oil
- ✧ 1 teaspoon garlic powder
- ✧ Salt and freshly ground black pepper, to taste
- ✧ 2 tablespoons grated Parmigiano cheese
- ✧ Lemon wedges, for serving

Directions

- ✧ Prepare Asparagus: Rinse the asparagus and dry thoroughly. In a mixing bowl, toss the asparagus with olive oil, garlic powder, salt, and pepper until well coated.
- ✧ Preheat Air Fryer: Set the air fryer to 400°F.
- ✧ Arrange in Basket: Place the asparagus spears in a single layer in the air fryer basket. Cook in batches if necessary to avoid overcrowding.
- ✧ Cooking Process: Cook for 8 minutes, or until the asparagus is tender and the edges begin to crisp up.
- ✧ Finish and Serve: Transfer the cooked asparagus to a serving plate, sprinkle with grated Parmigiano cheese, and serve with lemon wedges on the side.

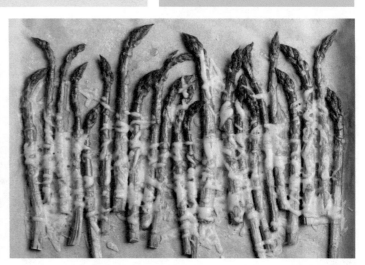

Nutritional values per serving - Calories: 85 Fat: 7 g Sodium: 75 mg Carbohydrates: 4 g Protein: 3 g

Crispy Eggplant Fries

 15' 15' 4 Easy

Eggplant is a versatile vegetable that perfectly absorbs flavors, making it ideal for experimenting with different seasonings. For a zesty twist, add a pinch of chili powder or swap smoked paprika for sumac to enhance the fries with a lemony undertone.

Ingredients

- 1 large eggplant, cut into 1/2-inch thick fries
- 1/4 cup olive oil
- 1/2 cup almond flour or breadcrumbs for a crunchier texture
- 1 teaspoon smoked paprika
- 1/2 teaspoon garlic powder
- Salt and freshly ground black pepper, to taste
- 1/4 cup grated Parmigiano cheese
- Fresh parsley, finely chopped (for garnish)

Directions

- Preheat Air Fryer: Set the air fryer to 380°F.
- Prepare Coating: In a shallow dish, mix almond flour or breadcrumbs with smoked paprika, garlic powder, salt, and black pepper.
- Coat Eggplant: Brush the eggplant fries with olive oil, then coat thoroughly in the breadcrumb mixture.
- Arrange in Basket: Place the eggplant fries in a single layer in the air fryer basket, avoiding overcrowding. Cook in batches if needed.
- Cooking Process: Cook for 15 minutes, flipping halfway through, until golden and crispy.
- Serve: Transfer the eggplant fries to a serving plate, sprinkle with grated Parmigiano and chopped parsley.

Nutritional values per serving - Calories: 210 Fat: 16 g Sodium: 200 mg Carbohydrates: 14 g Protein: 6 g

Ingredients

- 1 lb. fresh green beans, trimmed
- 2 tablespoons olive oil
- 1/2 cup almond flour or breadcrumbs for a crunchier texture
- 1 teaspoon garlic powder
- 1/2 teaspoon paprika
- Salt and freshly ground black pepper, to taste
- 2 tablespoons grated Parmigiano cheese (optional, for garnish)
- Fresh lemon wedges, for serving

Crispy Fried Green Beans

 10' 12' 4 Easy

Green beans are not just a summer pleasure but a year-round delight when cooked right. Sprinkle some crushed red pepper flakes before serving for those who enjoy a bit of spice, or drizzle with a balsamic glaze for a sweet and tangy finish.

Directions

- Coat Green Beans: In a large bowl, toss the green beans with olive oil to coat evenly.
- Prepare Coating: In a separate bowl, combine almond flour or breadcrumbs, garlic powder, paprika, salt, and black pepper.
- Dredge Green Beans: Dip the green beans in the breadcrumb mixture, coating them thoroughly.
- Preheat Air Fryer: Set the air fryer to 375°F.
- Arrange in Basket: Place the green beans in a single layer in the air fryer basket. Cook in batches if necessary to avoid overcrowding.
- Cooking Process: Air fry for 12 minutes or until the green beans are golden and crispy, shaking the basket halfway through.
- Finish and Serve: Serve hot, garnished with grated Parmigiano and lemon wedges on the side.

Nutritional values per serving - Calories: 160 Fat: 11 g Sodium: 120 mg Carbohydrates: 12 g Protein: 5 g

Ingredients

- 1 lb. carrots, peeled and sliced diagonally into 1/2-inch thick pieces
- 3 tablespoons olive oil
- 3 cloves garlic, minced
- 1 teaspoon dried thyme
- Salt and freshly ground black pepper, to taste
- Fresh parsley, finely chopped (for garnish)

Garlic Roasted Carrots

 10' 20' 4 🧑‍🍳 Easy

Roasting carrots intensifies their natural sweetness, making them a crowd-pleaser at any table. For an extra burst of flavor, sprinkle a dash of grated orange zest over the carrots before serving, which enhances the sweetness and adds a refreshing citrus note.

Directions

- Prepare Carrots: In a large bowl, toss the sliced carrots with olive oil, minced garlic, thyme, salt, and black pepper until evenly coated.
- Preheat Air Fryer: Set the air fryer to 380°F.
- Arrange in Basket: Place the carrots in a single layer in the air fryer basket, ensuring they are not overcrowded. Work in batches if necessary.
- Cooking Process: Cook for 20 minutes, shaking the basket halfway through, until the carrots are tender and the edges begin to caramelize.
- Serve: Transfer the roasted carrots to a serving platter and garnish with freshly chopped parsley.

Nutritional values per serving - Calories: 140 Fat: 10 g Sodium: 90 mg Carbohydrates: 12 g Protein: 1 g

Herbed Potato Wedges

 10' 25' 4 Easy

For a Mediterranean twist, try adding a pinch of sumac before serving for its lemony zest, or drizzle with a light tahini sauce. These herbed potato wedges pair wonderfully with both dips and main dishes, making them a versatile addition to any meal.

Ingredients

- 4 large potatoes, washed and cut into wedges
- 3 tablespoons olive oil
- 1 teaspoon dried rosemary
- 1 teaspoon dried thyme
- 1/2 teaspoon garlic powder
- Salt and freshly ground black pepper, to taste
- Fresh parsley, finely chopped (for garnish)
- Optional: Grated Parmigiano cheese for serving

Directions

- Season Potatoes: In a large bowl, toss the potato wedges with olive oil, rosemary, thyme, garlic powder, salt, and pepper until well coated.
- Preheat Air Fryer: Set the air fryer to 400°F.
- Arrange Wedges: Place the potato wedges in the air fryer basket in a single layer to ensure even cooking. Work in batches if necessary.
- Cooking Process: Cook for 25 minutes, shaking the basket halfway through, until the potatoes are golden brown and crispy.
- Serve: Garnish the hot potato wedges with chopped parsley and a sprinkle of grated Parmigiano, if desired.

Nutritional values per serving - Calories: 280 Fat: 10 g Sodium: 70 mg Carbohydrates: 44 g Protein: 6 g

Lemon Garlic Asparagus

 5'   8'   4   Easy

Asparagus is not only delightful when crisp, but it's also a treasure trove of vitamins. For an extra layer of flavor, try drizzling with a balsamic reduction after cooking, which complements the fresh zestiness of the lemon and the robust aroma of garlic.

Ingredients

- ◇ 1 lb. fresh asparagus, ends trimmed
- ◇ 2 tablespoons olive oil
- ◇ 3 cloves garlic, minced
- ◇ Zest and juice of 1 lemon
- ◇ Salt and freshly ground black pepper, to taste
- ◇ Optional: A sprinkle of crushed red pepper flakes

Directions

- ◇ Prepare Asparagus: In a mixing bowl, toss the asparagus with olive oil, minced garlic, lemon zest, lemon juice, salt, and black pepper until well coated.
- ◇ Preheat Air Fryer: Set the air fryer to 380°F.
- ◇ Arrange Asparagus: Place the asparagus in the air fryer basket in a single layer to ensure even cooking.
- ◇ Cooking Process: Cook for 8 minutes, or until the asparagus is tender and lightly browned on the edges.
- ◇ Serve: Serve the asparagus immediately, optionally sprinkled with red pepper flakes for a hint of spice.

Nutritional values per serving - Calories: 90 Fat: 7 g Sodium: 75 mg Carbohydrates: 6 g Protein: 3 g

Ingredients

- ◇ 1 lb. fresh green beans, ends trimmed
- ◇ 2 tablespoons olive oil
- ◇ 1/2 cup grated Parmigiano cheese
- ◇ 2 cloves garlic, minced
- ◇ Salt and freshly ground black pepper, to taste
- ◇ Optional: A pinch of crushed red pepper flakes for heat

Parmesan Green Beans

 5'   10'   4   Easy

A simple twist on traditional steamed green beans, this dish brings out a rich, nutty flavor that only Parmigiano can offer. For those who enjoy a bit of texture, add some toasted slivered almonds or breadcrumbs for the final two minutes of air frying for a delightful crunch.

Directions

- ◇ Prepare Green Beans: In a large bowl, toss the green beans with olive oil, minced garlic, salt, and pepper until well coated.
- ◇ Preheat Air Fryer: Set the air fryer to 375°F.
- ◇ Cook Green Beans: Spread the green beans in a single layer in the air fryer basket. Cook for 10 minutes, shaking halfway through, until tender and slightly crispy.
- ◇ Add Cheese: Transfer the cooked green beans to a serving dish, sprinkle with grated Parmigiano cheese, and toss to melt the cheese.
- ◇ Serve: Serve immediately, optionally sprinkled with red pepper flakes for added spice.

Nutritional values per serving - Calories: 150 Fat: 11 g Sodium: 220 mg Carbohydrates: 9 g Protein: 6 g

Ingredients

- 2 cups cooked risotto, cooled (Ch. 8)
- 1/2 cup grated Parmigiano cheese
- 1/4 cup finely chopped fresh basil
- 1 egg, beaten
- 1/2 cup all-purpose flour
- 1 cup breadcrumbs
- Salt and freshly ground black pepper, to taste
- Olive oil spray

Parmesan Risotto Balls

 15' 20' 4 👨‍🍳 Medium

For a delightful twist, add a cube of mozzarella inside each risotto ball before breading, which will melt into a gooey center as they cook. This simple addition transforms each bite into a creamy surprise, marrying well with the crisp outer shell and herb-infused risotto.

Directions

- **Mix Ingredients:** In a large bowl, mix the cooled risotto with Parmigiano cheese, chopped basil, and beaten egg. Season with salt and pepper.
- **Form Balls:** Shape the risotto mixture into small balls, about the size of a golf ball.
- **Coating Setup:** Place flour, a second beaten egg, and breadcrumbs in three separate shallow dishes.
- **Coat Balls:** Roll each risotto ball in flour, dip in egg, then coat thoroughly in breadcrumbs.
- **Preheat Air Fryer:** Set the air fryer to 350°F and lightly spray the basket with olive oil spray.
- **Arrange in Basket:** Place the risotto balls in the basket without touching. Cook in batches if needed. Spray the balls with olive oil.
- **Cook:** Cook for 10-12 minutes, or until golden and crispy, shaking the basket halfway through.
- **Serve:** Serve warm with marinara sauce (Ch. 8) or your preferred dipping sauce.

Nutritional values per serving - Calories: 290 Fat: 8 g Sodium: 320 mg Carbohydrates: 42 g Protein: 10 g

Roasted Vegetables with Olive Oil and Herbs

 10' 20' 4 👨‍🍳 Easy

Infuse a Mediterranean flair by finishing the dish with a sprinkle of crumbled feta cheese just before serving. The warmth of the vegetables slightly melts the feta, creating a creamy texture that contrasts beautifully with the crisp veggies.

Ingredients

- 1 zucchini, cut into bite-sized pieces
- 1 yellow squash, cut into bite-sized pieces
- 1 red bell pepper, seeded and cut into chunks
- 1 yellow bell pepper, seeded and cut into chunks
- 1 small red onion, cut into wedges
- 2 carrots, sliced
- 2 tablespoons extra virgin olive oil
- 1 teaspoon dried oregano
- 1 teaspoon dried basil
- 1/2 teaspoon garlic powder
- Salt and freshly ground black pepper, to taste
- Fresh parsley, chopped (for garnish)

Directions

- **Prepare Vegetables:** In a large bowl, combine zucchini, yellow squash, bell peppers, onion, and carrots. Drizzle with olive oil and sprinkle with oregano, basil, garlic powder, salt, and pepper. Toss well to coat.
- **Preheat Air Fryer:** Set the air fryer to 380°F.
- **Arrange in Basket:** Place the vegetables in a single layer in the air fryer basket. Cook in batches to prevent overcrowding.
- **Cooking Process:** Air fry for about 15-20 minutes, shaking the basket halfway through, until the vegetables are tender and caramelized.
- **Serve:** Transfer the vegetables to a serving dish and garnish with chopped fresh parsley.

Nutritional values per serving - Calories: 120 Fat: 7 g Sodium: 70 mg Carbohydrates: 13 g Protein: 2 g

Spiced Carrot Fries

 10' 18' 4 Easy

For an extra touch of zest, serve these spiced carrot fries with a side of yogurt dipping sauce (Ch. 8) mixed with fresh dill and a squeeze of lemon. The cool, creamy sauce complements the spices beautifully, making each bite a delightful contrast.

Ingredients

- 6 large carrots, peeled and cut into thin sticks
- 2 tablespoons olive oil
- 1 teaspoon ground cumin
- 1/2 teaspoon paprika
- 1/4 teaspoon ground coriander
- 1/4 teaspoon turmeric
- Salt and freshly ground black pepper, to taste
- Fresh parsley, finely chopped (for garnish)

Directions

- Season Carrots: In a large bowl, toss the carrot sticks with olive oil, cumin, paprika, coriander, turmeric, salt, and pepper until well coated.
- Preheat Air Fryer: Set the air fryer to 380°F.
- Arrange in Basket: Place the carrot fries in a single layer in the air fryer basket. Work in batches to prevent overcrowding.
- Cooking Process: Air fry for 15-18 minutes, shaking the basket halfway through, until the carrot fries are tender and edges start to crisp.
- Serve: Transfer the carrot fries to a serving plate and garnish with chopped parsley.

Nutritional values per serving - Calories: 105 Fat: 7 g Sodium: 120 mg Carbohydrates: 10 g Protein: 1 g.

Stuffed Artichokes

Ingredients

- 4 large artichokes
- 1 cup Italian breadcrumbs (Ch. 8)
- 1/2 cup grated Parmigiano cheese
- 3 cloves garlic, minced
- 1/4 cup chopped fresh parsley
- Zest of 1 lemon
- 1/4 cup olive oil, plus extra for drizzling
- Salt and black pepper, to taste
- Lemon wedges, for serving

 20' 22' 4 Medium

To add a twist to this classic dish, mix in some finely chopped sun-dried tomatoes or olives into the breadcrumb stuffing. It'll infuse the artichokes with a vibrant burst of Mediterranean flavors that pair beautifully with a crisp white wine.

Directions

- Prepare Artichokes: Trim the stems and remove the tough outer leaves from the artichokes. Cut off the top third to expose the inner leaves and remove the choke if present.
- Make Stuffing: In a bowl, combine breadcrumbs, Parmigiano cheese, garlic, parsley, lemon zest, olive oil, salt, and pepper.
- Stuff Artichokes: Generously fill the spaces between the artichoke leaves with the breadcrumb mixture.
- Preheat Air Fryer: Set the air fryer to 360°F.
- Arrange Artichokes: Place the stuffed artichokes in the air fryer basket and drizzle with additional olive oil.
- Cooking Process: Air fry for 20-22 minutes, or until the artichokes are tender and the stuffing is golden brown.
- Serve: Enjoy the artichokes hot, accompanied by lemon wedges for squeezing.

Nutritional values per serving - Calories: 290 Fat: 17 g Sodium: 410 mg Carbohydrates: 28 g Protein: 8 g

Chapter 5. Seafood Delights

Ah, the bountiful seas! As an Italian chef nurtured by the vibrant shores of Genoa, the ocean's treasure trove of flavors has always been close to my heart—and my kitchen. The aroma of fresh fish grilling as the sun sets over the Mediterranean is a fond memory that, like a cherished recipe, I carry with me. Seafood, with its delicate textures and flavors, has always demanded a respect for tradition and a touch of culinary finesse.

Now, as we embrace the air frying revolution, I'm delighted to show how this modern marvel can transform seafood into dishes that are both spectacularly delicious and wonderfully healthy. Air frying offers a way to enjoy the beloved crispiness of fried seafood without the heaviness of oil, preserving the sublime natural flavors of the sea.

In this chapter, we will dive into recipes that are steeped in Mediterranean tradition yet innovatively adapted for the air fryer. From crispy calamari to tender scallops, and robust tuna steaks to delicate shrimp, each recipe is designed to elevate your dining experience. The air fryer not only simplifies the cooking process but enhances it, allowing the natural flavors of the seafood to shine through complemented by a variety of herbs and spices that echo the essence of the Mediterranean coast.

Join me as we explore how traditional seafood dishes can be transformed with a touch of modern convenience, ensuring that each meal is a celebration of flavor and a testament to the joys of healthy eating. Whether you're a seasoned fisherman or a casual cook, these recipes will bring the freshness of the sea straight to your table, with all the zest and zeal of Italian cooking. Let's set sail on this culinary journey together, embracing both the old and the new with open arms and eager palates.

Air-Fried Calamari

 15'   10'   4 Easy

Dive into the heart of the Mediterranean with each bite of these crispy calamari. For a zesty twist, sprinkle a pinch of sumac over the cooked calamari before serving, adding a lemony tang that elevates this classic seaside fare.

Ingredients

- 1 lb. calamari, cleaned and cut into rings
- 1 cup all-purpose flour
- 2 teaspoons paprika
- 1 teaspoon garlic powder
- 1/2 teaspoon salt
- 1/4 teaspoon black pepper
- 1/2 cup milk
- Lemon wedges, for serving
- Fresh parsley, chopped (for garnish)

Directions

- Mix Coating: In a shallow bowl, combine the flour, paprika, garlic powder, salt, and black pepper.
- Coat Calamari: Dip calamari rings first in milk, then dredge in the flour mixture until well coated.
- Preheat Air Fryer: Set the air fryer to 400°F.
- Arrange Calamari: Place the coated calamari rings in a single layer in the air fryer basket. Avoid overcrowding and work in batches if necessary for even cooking.
- Cooking Process: Cook for 8-10 minutes, shaking the basket halfway through, until the calamari is golden and crispy.
- Serve and Garnish: Serve the calamari hot, garnished with chopped parsley and lemon wedges on the side.

Nutritional values per serving - Calories: 235 Fat: 4 g Sodium: 340 mg Carbohydrates: 34 g Protein: 18 g

Blackened Tilapia

 10' 10' 4 Easy

For those who love a touch of heat, the cayenne pepper in this recipe brings a delightful kick, enhancing the tilapia's mild flavor. Pair with a cool yogurt-based dip (Ch. 8) or a squeeze of fresh lime for an extra layer of flavor. This dish is a testament to the beauty of simplicity in Mediterranean cooking.

Ingredients

- 4 tilapia fillets (about 6 oz each)
- 2 tablespoons olive oil
- 1 tablespoon paprika
- 1 teaspoon garlic powder
- 1 teaspoon onion powder
- 1 teaspoon dried thyme
- 1 teaspoon dried oregano
- 1/2 teaspoon cayenne pepper (adjust to taste)
- Salt and black pepper to taste
- Lemon wedges, for serving

Directions

- Prepare Seasoning Mix: In a small bowl, mix paprika, garlic powder, onion powder, thyme, oregano, cayenne pepper, salt, and black pepper.
- Season Fillets: Brush each tilapia fillet with olive oil, then apply the spice mixture generously on both sides.
- Preheat Air Fryer: Set the air fryer to 400°F.
- Arrange Fillets: Place the seasoned tilapia in the air fryer basket in a single layer to avoid overlap. Cook in batches if necessary.
- Cooking Process: Air fry for 10 minutes or until the fish is flaky and the exterior is crisp.
- Serve: Offer immediately with fresh lemon wedges alongside.

Nutritional values per serving - Calories: 210 Fat: 12 g Sodium: 75 mg Carbohydrates: 2 g Protein: 23 g

Clams with Herb Crust

Ingredients

- 24 littleneck clams, scrubbed clean
- 1 cup Italian breadcrumbs (Ch. 8)
- 1/4 cup grated Parmigiano cheese
- 3 tablespoons fresh parsley, finely chopped
- 2 cloves garlic, minced
- Zest of 1 lemon
- 4 tablespoons olive oil
- Salt and pepper, to taste
- Lemon wedges, for serving

 15'  10' 4 Easy

For an aromatic twist, add a sprinkle of crushed red pepper to the breadcrumb mixture for a hint of heat, complementing the briny sweetness of the clams perfectly. This dish marries the deep flavors of the sea with the crisp, golden texture of the breadcrumbs, making it a festive choice for any seafood lover.

Directions

- Preheat Air Fryer: Set your air fryer to 380°F.
- Cook Clams: Arrange the clams in a single layer in the air fryer basket. Cook for 2-3 minutes or just until they start to open.
- Prepare Herb Crust: While the clams are cooking, mix breadcrumbs, Parmigiano, parsley, garlic, lemon zest, olive oil, and a pinch of salt and pepper in a bowl.
- Stuff Clams: Remove clams from the air fryer once they begin to open. Pry them fully open (discard any that do not open) and top each with the herb crust mixture.
- Cook Stuffed Clams: Return the stuffed clams to the air fryer basket. Cook for another 5-7 minutes or until the topping is golden and crispy.
- Serve: Present immediately with lemon wedges alongside.

Nutritional values per serving - Calories: 250 Fat: 12 g Sodium: 350 mg Carbohydrates: 20 g Protein: 15 g

Ingredients

- 1 lb. large shrimp, peeled and deveined
- 1/2 cup all-purpose flour
- 1/2 teaspoon paprika
- 1/4 teaspoon garlic powder
- Salt and black pepper to taste
- 2 large eggs, beaten
- 1 cup shredded coconut
- 1/2 cup panko breadcrumbs
- Olive oil spray

For the Dipping Sauce:

- 1/2 cup orange marmalade
- 1 tablespoon lime juice
- 1/2 teaspoon crushed red pepper flakes

Coconut Shrimp

 15' 8' 4 Easy

For a zesty twist, add a pinch of curry powder to the coconut and breadcrumb mixture. This will imbue your shrimp with a subtle exotic flavor that beautifully complements the sweetness of the coconut.

Directions

- Prepare Coating: In a shallow bowl, combine flour, paprika, garlic powder, salt, and black pepper. In another bowl, mix shredded coconut and panko breadcrumbs.
- Coat Shrimp: Dredge each shrimp first in the flour mixture, then in beaten eggs, and finally in the coconut-breadcrumb mixture.
- Preheat Air Fryer: Set the air fryer to 400°F and spray the basket with olive oil.
- Arrange Shrimp: Place the shrimp in a single layer in the basket, ensuring they do not touch. Spray the shrimp lightly with olive oil.
- Cook: Air fry for about 8 minutes, flipping halfway through, until the shrimp are golden and crispy.
- Prepare Dipping Sauce: Mix orange marmalade, lime juice, and crushed red pepper flakes in a small bowl.
- Serve: Offer the shrimp hot with the spicy citrus dipping sauce on the side.

Nutritional values per serving - Calories: 410 Fat: 12 g Sodium: 470 mg Carbohydrates: 53 g Protein: 25 g

Cod Fish Tacos

 15' 10' 4 Easy

Add a zestful twist to your tacos by drizzling them with a homemade chipotle lime sauce (Ch. 8). Simply blend one chipotle pepper in adobo sauce with the juice of one lime and a bit of sour cream for a smoky, tangy kick that complements the spices on the fish beautifully.

Ingredients

- 4 cod fillets (about 6 oz each)
- 1 tablespoon olive oil
- 1 teaspoon smoked paprika
- 1 teaspoon garlic powder
- 1 teaspoon ground cumin
- Salt and pepper, to taste
- 8 small flour tortillas
- 1 avocado, sliced
- 1/2 red onion, thinly sliced
- 1/2 cup fresh cilantro, chopped
- 1 lime, cut into wedges
- 1/2 cup sour cream
- 1 cup shredded cabbage

Directions

- Preheat the air fryer to 400°F.
- Brush each cod fillet with olive oil. In a small bowl, mix smoked paprika, garlic powder, cumin, salt, and pepper. Sprinkle the spice mixture evenly over the cod fillets.
- Place the cod in the air fryer basket, ensuring they are not overlapping. Cook for about 10 minutes, or until the fish is cooked through and flakes easily with a fork.
- Once the fish is cooked, remove it from the air fryer and cover to keep warm. Place tortillas in the air fryer and warm for 1-2 minutes until soft and pliable.
- To assemble the tacos, flake the cod with a fork and divide it among the warmed tortillas. Top with avocado slices, red onion, shredded cabbage, and cilantro.
- Serve each taco with a wedge of lime and a dollop of sour cream on the side.

Nutritional values per serving - Calories: 350 Fat: 15 g Sodium: 400 mg Carbohydrates: 28 g Protein: 28 g

Crab Cakes with Aioli

 20' 10' 4 Easy

For an extra layer of flavor, mix a pinch of finely chopped capers into the aioli. This adds a delightful briny contrast to the sweet, tender crab, enhancing the overall depth of your dish.

Nutritional values per serving - Calories: 320 Fat: 18 g Sodium: 760 mg Carbohydrates: 12 g Protein: 24 g

Ingredients

- 1 lb. crab meat, picked over for shells
- 1/2 cup breadcrumbs
- 1/4 cup finely chopped green onions
- 1/4 cup finely chopped red bell pepper
- 1 egg, beaten
- 2 tablespoons mayonnaise
- 1 tablespoon Dijon mustard
- 1 teaspoon Old Bay seasoning
- 1/2 teaspoon garlic powder
- Salt and black pepper to taste
- 1/4 cup all-purpose flour, for dusting
- Olive oil spray

For the Aioli:

- 1/2 cup mayonnaise
- 1 clove garlic, minced
- 1 tablespoon lemon juice
- 1 teaspoon Dijon mustard
- Salt and pepper to taste

Directions

- **Mix Ingredients:** In a large bowl, combine crab meat, breadcrumbs, green onions, red bell pepper, egg, mayonnaise, Dijon mustard, Old Bay seasoning, garlic powder, salt, and pepper. Gently mix until thoroughly combined.
- **Form Patties:** Shape the mixture into 8 equal-sized patties and dust each lightly with flour.
- **Preheat Air Fryer:** Preheat the air fryer to 375°F and spray the basket with olive oil.
- **Cook Crab Cakes:** Place the crab cakes in the basket, ensuring they don't touch. Spray tops with olive oil. Cook for 10 minutes, flipping once, until golden and crispy.
- **Prepare Aioli:** While the crab cakes are cooking, mix all aioli ingredients in a small bowl until smooth.
- **Serve:** Serve the crab cakes warm, topped with or accompanied by aioli for dipping.

Ingredients

- 4 white fish fillets (such as cod or haddock, about 6 oz each)
- 1 cup all-purpose flour
- 1 teaspoon baking powder
- 1 teaspoon paprika
- 1/2 teaspoon garlic powder
- Salt and black pepper to taste
- 1 cup cold sparkling water
- 3 large russet potatoes, peeled and cut into fries
- Olive oil spray
- Lemon wedges and tartar sauce (Ch. 8), for serving

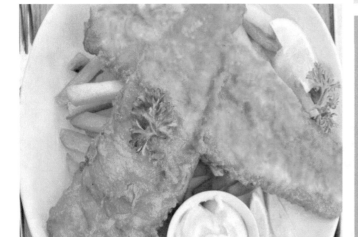

Nutritional values per serving - Calories: 450 Fat: 12 g Sodium: 280 mg Carbohydrates: 55 g Protein: 32 g

Fish and Chips

 20' 22' 4 Easy

Enhance the flavor of your fish and chips by adding a pinch of turmeric to the batter, not only for a delightful hint of spice but also for a vibrant golden hue that makes the dish visually appealing. This addition infuses a touch of Mediterranean flair into this classic British dish.

Directions

- **Prepare Batter:** In a large bowl, combine flour, baking powder, paprika, garlic powder, salt, and black pepper. Gradually whisk in cold sparkling water until smooth.
- **Batter Fish:** Dip each fish fillet into the batter, ensuring it is completely coated.
- **Preheat Air Fryer:** Set the air fryer to 400°F and spray the basket with olive oil spray.
- **Cook Fish:** Place the battered fish in the air fryer basket without overlapping. Spray the tops with additional oil. Cook for 10-12 minutes, flipping halfway through, until golden and crispy.
- **Prepare Fries:** Toss fries with olive oil and salt. After cooking the fish, air fry the fries at 400°F for 10-12 minutes, shaking halfway through until golden.
- **Serve:** Present the air-fried fish and chips hot with lemon wedges and tartar sauce.

Garlic and Paprika Shrimp

 10' 8' 4 Easy

For an extra kick, sprinkle a pinch of chili flakes over the shrimp before cooking to add a subtle heat that complements the smoky paprika beautifully. This dish is perfect for a quick, flavorful meal that brings a taste of the Mediterranean right to your table, showing how simple ingredients can create a feast for the senses.

Ingredients

- 1 lb. large shrimp, peeled and deveined
- 2 tablespoons olive oil
- 3 cloves garlic, minced
- 1 teaspoon smoked paprika
- 1/2 teaspoon ground cumin
- Salt and freshly ground black pepper, to taste
- 1 tablespoon fresh parsley, finely chopped
- Lemon wedges, for serving

Directions

- Prepare Marinade: In a large bowl, combine olive oil, minced garlic, smoked paprika, cumin, salt, and black pepper. Mix well.
- Marinate Shrimp: Add shrimp to the marinade and toss to coat evenly. Let marinate for about 10 minutes at room temperature.
- Preheat Air Fryer: Set the air fryer to 400°F. Arrange shrimp in a single layer in the basket, avoiding overcrowding.
- Cook Shrimp: Air fry for 8 minutes, turning halfway through, until shrimp are cooked and slightly crisp.
- Serve: Garnish with freshly chopped parsley and accompany with lemon wedges.

Nutritional values per serving - Calories: 180 Fat: 8 g Sodium: 220 mg Carbohydrates: 2 g Protein: 23 g

Grilled Octopus with Lemon and Olive Oil

 10'* 12' 4 Mediur

* plus marinating time

For an even richer flavor, sprinkle some crushed red pepper flakes into the marinade for a slight heat that complements the freshness of the lemon. This dish is a fantastic way to enjoy a classic Mediterranean flavor using the air fryer, highlighting how traditional ingredients can be transformed into modern culinary delights.

Ingredients

- 2 lbs. pre-cooked octopus tentacles (Ch. 8)
- 1/4 cup extra-virgin olive oil
- 2 lemons, 1 juiced and 1 cut into wedges
- 3 cloves garlic, minced
- 1 teaspoon dried oregano
- Fresh parsley, finely chopped for garnish
- Salt and freshly ground black pepper, to taste

Directions

- Prepare Marinade: In a bowl, combine olive oil, lemon juice, minced garlic, oregano, salt, and black pepper. Mix well.
- Marinate Octopus: Add octopus tentacles to the marinade, ensuring they are well coated. Marinate for at least 30 minutes in the refrigerator.
- Preheat Air Fryer: Set the air fryer to 400°F.
- Cook Octopus: Place marinated octopus in the air fryer basket. Air fry for 12 minutes, turning halfway, until edges are slightly crisp.
- Serve: Garnish with freshly chopped parsley and lemon wedges.

Nutritional values per serving - Calories: 250 Fat: 15 g Sodium: 580 mg Carbohydrates: 5 g Protein: 25 g

Herb-Crusted Cod

 10' 12' 4 Easy

For a delightful twist, try mixing a little grated Parmigiano into the breadcrumb mix before coating the fish. It adds a savory depth that beautifully complements the fresh herbs and lemon.

Ingredients

- ✧ 4 cod fillets (about 6 oz each)
- ✧ 1/2 cup panko breadcrumbs
- ✧ 1/4 cup finely chopped fresh parsley
- ✧ 2 tablespoons fresh basil, finely chopped
- ✧ 2 cloves garlic, minced
- ✧ Zest of 1 lemon
- ✧ 2 tablespoons olive oil
- ✧ Salt and freshly ground black pepper, to taste
- ✧ Lemon wedges, for serving

Directions

- ✧ Prepare Breadcrumb Mix: In a small bowl, mix panko breadcrumbs, parsley, basil, garlic, and lemon zest. Drizzle with 1 tablespoon olive oil until well coated.
- ✧ Season Cod: Pat cod fillets dry and season both sides with salt and pepper.
- ✧ Add Crust: Brush remaining olive oil over each cod fillet, then press the herb breadcrumb mixture onto the top to form a crust.
- ✧ Preheat Air Fryer: Set air fryer to 400°F.
- ✧ Arrange in Basket: Place cod fillets in the basket, crusted side up, without overlapping.
- ✧ Cook: Air fry for 12 minutes, until crust is golden and fish flakes easily with a fork.
- ✧ Serve: Offer immediately with lemon wedges.

Nutritional values per serving - Calories: 220 Fat: 8 g Sodium: 180 mg Carbohydrates: 10 g Protein: 23 g

Ingredients

- ✧ 1 lb. large shrimp, peeled and deveined
- ✧ 1/2 cup homemade or store-bought pesto sauce (Ch. 8)
- ✧ 1 tablespoon olive oil
- ✧ 1 teaspoon lemon zest
- ✧ 2 tablespoons lemon juice
- ✧ Salt and freshly ground black pepper, to taste
- ✧ 8 wooden skewers, soaked in water for 30 minutes

Pesto Shrimp Skewers

 15' 8' 4 Easy

Enhance the Mediterranean flair by adding some chopped sun-dried tomatoes to the pesto mixture before marinating. It infuses the shrimp with a sweet, tangy flavor that's utterly delightful on the palate.

Directions

- ✧ Mix Ingredients: In a large bowl, combine shrimp, pesto, olive oil, lemon zest, and lemon juice. Season with salt and pepper, then toss to evenly coat.
- ✧ Skewer Shrimp: Thread shrimp onto soaked skewers, packing tightly.
- ✧ Preheat Air Fryer: Set air fryer to 400°F.
- ✧ Arrange Skewers: Place shrimp skewers in the air fryer basket in a single layer without touching each other.
- ✧ Cook: Air fry for about 8 minutes, turning halfway through, until shrimp are pink and fully cooked.
- ✧ Serve: Present skewers hot, garnished with additional lemon wedges and fresh herbs.

Nutritional values per serving - Calories: 210 Fat: 12 g Sodium: 560 mg Carbohydrates: 3 g Protein: 24 g

Ingredients

- 1 lb. cooked salmon, flaked
- 1 large egg, beaten
- 1/4 cup breadcrumbs
- 2 tablespoons mayonnaise
- 1 tablespoon Dijon mustard
- 1 tablespoon fresh dill, chopped
- 1 teaspoon lemon zest
- Salt and black pepper, to taste
- 2 tablespoons olive oil for brushing
- Lemon wedges, for

Salmon Croquettes

 20'   15'   4 Easy

For a spicy twist, add a pinch of smoked paprika to the salmon mixture before forming the croquettes. It adds a lovely warmth and color, enhancing the deep flavors of the salmon.

Directions

- **Prepare Salmon Mixture:** In a large bowl, combine flaked salmon, egg, breadcrumbs, mayonnaise, Dijon mustard, dill, and lemon zest. Season with salt and pepper and mix until thoroughly combined.
- **Form Patties:** Shape the mixture into 8 equal-sized patties.
- **Preheat Air Fryer:** Set air fryer to 375°F.
- **Arrange Croquettes:** Brush each salmon croquette lightly with olive oil on both sides. Place in the air fryer basket in a single layer without touching.
- **Cook:** Air fry for 15 minutes, flipping halfway through, until croquettes are golden and crispy.
- **Serve:** Offer croquettes hot with lemon wedges on the side for squeezing over.

Nutritional values per serving - Calories: 290 Fat: 18 g Sodium: 320 mg Carbohydrates: 7 g Protein: 23 g

Scallops with Lemon Garlic Sauce

 10'   10'   4   Easy

To add a bit of crunch and extra flavor, sprinkle some finely grated Parmigiano over the scallops just before serving. The heat from the scallops will slightly melt the cheese, creating a delightful texture and rich taste.

Ingredients

- 16 large sea scallops, patted dry
- 2 tablespoons olive oil
- Salt and black pepper, to taste
- 4 cloves garlic, minced
- Juice of 1 lemon
- 2 tablespoons unsalted butter
- 1 tablespoon chopped fresh parsley
- Lemon slices, for garnish

Directions

- **Preheat Air Fryer:** Set the air fryer to 400°F.
- **Season Scallops:** Toss the scallops with 1 tablespoon of olive oil, salt, and pepper.
- **Cook Scallops:** Arrange in a single layer in the air fryer basket and cook for 8-10 minutes, or until golden and opaque.
- **Prepare Sauce:** While scallops cook, heat the remaining olive oil in a skillet over medium heat. Sauté minced garlic until fragrant, about 1 minute.
- **Finish Sauce:** Add lemon juice and butter to the skillet, stirring until butter melts and the sauce is combined.
- **Serve:** Drizzle lemon garlic sauce over the cooked scallops, sprinkle with chopped parsley, and garnish with lemon slices.

Nutritional values per serving - Calories: 220 Fat: 15 g Sodium: 480 mg Carbohydrates: 3 g Protein: 20 g

Stuffed Squid

 20' 15' 4 Medium

For a delightful twist, mix some finely chopped sun-dried tomatoes into the stuffing for a burst of Mediterranean flavor. This not only adds color but also enhances the squid with a sweet, tangy taste that pairs wonderfully with the subtle oceanic flavor.

Ingredients

- 8 small squid, bodies cleaned and tentacles reserved
- 1/2 cup breadcrumbs
- 1/4 cup finely chopped parsley
- 2 cloves garlic, minced
- 1/4 cup grated Parmigiano cheese
- 1/4 teaspoon red pepper flakes
- Salt and black pepper, to taste
- 2 tablespoons olive oil
- Lemon wedges, for serving

Directions

- ✧ Preheat Air Fryer: Set the air fryer to 360°F.
- ✧ Prepare Tentacles: Finely chop the reserved squid tentacles.
- ✧ Mix Filling: In a bowl, combine breadcrumbs, parsley, garlic, Parmigiano, red pepper flakes, chopped tentacles, salt, and black pepper.
- ✧ Stuff Squid: Fill squid bodies with the breadcrumb mixture, securing the open ends with toothpicks.
- ✧ Prepare for Cooking: Brush the stuffed squid with olive oil and place in the air fryer basket.
- ✧ Cook: Air fry for 15 minutes, or until the squid is tender and the filling is golden.
- ✧ Serve: Present hot with lemon wedges on the side.

Nutritional values per serving - Calories: 210 Fat: 10 g Sodium: 340 mg Carbohydrates: 12 g Protein: 18 g

Ingredients

- 4 tilapia fillets (about 6 oz each)
- 2 tablespoons olive oil
- 1 lemon, thinly sliced
- 2 tablespoons fresh dill, chopped
- Salt and black pepper, to taste
- 1/4 teaspoon garlic powder
- Lemon wedges, for serving

Tilapia with Lemon and Dill

 10' 12' 4 Easy

For a touch of Italian flair, add a sprinkle of capers along with the lemon and dill before cooking. This will infuse the tilapia with a lovely, briny contrast that complements the freshness of the lemon and dill beautifully.

Directions

- ✧ Preheat Air Fryer: Set the air fryer to 360°F.
- ✧ Prepare Tilapia: Pat the tilapia fillets dry, brush with olive oil, and season with salt, black pepper, and garlic powder.
- ✧ Arrange in Basket: Place lemon slices in a single layer in the basket and top with the seasoned tilapia.
- ✧ Add Dill: Sprinkle chopped dill over the fillets.
- ✧ Cook: Air fry for 10-12 minutes, until the fish flakes easily with a fork.
- ✧ Serve: Present immediately with additional lemon wedges on the side.

Nutritional values per serving - Calories: 190 Fat: 10 g Sodium: 125 mg Carbohydrates: 2 g Protein: 23 g

Ingredients

- 2 cans (5 oz each) tuna in water, drained and flaked
- 1/4 cup breadcrumbs
- 1/4 cup finely chopped red onion
- 2 tablespoons chopped fresh parsley
- 1 garlic clove, minced
- 1 large egg, beaten
- Zest of 1 lemon
- 1 tablespoon lemon juice
- 1/2 teaspoon paprika
- Salt and black pepper, to taste
- Olive oil spray

TUNA PATTIES

 15'   10'   4 Easy

Adding a pinch of sumac to the patties gives them a slight tangy flavor that pairs wonderfully with the lemon zest. This spice is not just for flavor; it's also packed with antioxidants, making these tuna patties not only delicious but also a healthier option for a quick meal.

Directions

- Mix Ingredients: In a large bowl, combine tuna, breadcrumbs, red onion, parsley, garlic, egg, lemon zest, lemon juice, paprika, salt, and pepper.
- Form Patties: Shape the mixture into eight small patties.
- Preheat Air Fryer: Set the air fryer to 400°F.
- Prepare Basket: Lightly spray the air fryer basket with olive oil, place the patties in the basket without touching, and spray the tops with olive oil.
- Cook Patties: Cook for 10 minutes, flipping halfway, until golden brown and cooked through.
- Serve: Present hot, optionally garnished with additional parsley.

Nutritional values per serving - Calories: 180 Fat: 6 g Sodium: 290 mg Carbohydrates: 8 g Protein: 23 g

TUNA STEAKS WITH CAPER SAUCE

 10'   8'   4   Easy

For an Italian twist, mix a pinch of dried oregano into your caper sauce. Oregano not only enhances the flavor with a touch of the Mediterranean but also offers powerful antioxidants and anti-inflammatory properties, making this dish as healthful as it is flavorful.

Ingredients

- 4 tuna steaks (about 6 oz each)
- 2 tablespoons olive oil
- Salt and freshly ground black pepper, to taste
- 1/4 cup finely chopped shallots
- 2 cloves garlic, minced
- 1/4 cup white wine
- 2 tablespoons capers, rinsed
- 1 tablespoon lemon juice
- 1 tablespoon chopped fresh parsley
- Lemon wedges, for serving

Directions

- Preheat Air Fryer: Set the air fryer to 400°F.
- Prepare Tuna: Brush both sides of the tuna steaks with olive oil and season with salt and pepper.
- Arrange in Basket: Place the tuna steaks in the air fryer basket, ensuring no overlap.
- Cook: Air fry for 6-8 minutes, adjusting time based on the thickness of the steaks, until desired doneness is achieved.
- Make Sauce: While tuna cooks, heat a small pan, sauté shallots and garlic in olive oil until translucent, about 2 minutes. Deglaze with white wine, add capers, and simmer until sauce reduces slightly, 3-4 minutes. Stir in lemon juice and parsley.
- Serve: Drizzle caper sauce over the cooked tuna steaks and accompany with a lemon wedge.

Nutritional values per serving - Calories: 280 Fat: 12 g Sodium: 320 mg Carbohydrates: 3 g Protein: 40 g

Chapter 6. Vegetarian Delicacies

In this delightful chapter, we embrace the vibrant and nourishing world of vegetarian cuisine through the innovative lens of air frying. As a chef whose heart beats to the rhythm of traditional Mediterranean kitchens, I have always cherished the abundant use of vegetables and legumes that typify our diet—a testament to both our love for the earth's bounty and our respect for its sustainability.

Yet, even for a steadfast advocate of the old ways like myself, the air fryer has revealed itself as a remarkable companion in the kitchen. It allows us to celebrate the natural flavors and textures of vegetables without the need for excessive oil, preserving their nutrients and enhancing their natural colors.

Whether you are a seasoned vegetarian or simply looking to incorporate more plant-based meals into your diet, this chapter promises to transform how you view and prepare vegetables. From the crispy, golden edges of air-fried butternut squash to the tender, herbed delights of stuffed zucchini boats, each recipe is designed to satisfy the palate and nourish the body.

With each dish, we aim not only to feed but to inspire, offering up a way to connect with the ingredients and the cooking process deeply. As we explore these vegetarian delicacies, crafted to suit the air fryer's unique capabilities, we invite both traditionalists and modern culinary adventurers to join in the celebration of flavor and innovation. Embrace these recipes with an open heart and a ready fork, and discover just how delicious healthy eating can be!

Ingredients

- ✧ 1 medium butternut squash, peeled and cut into 1-inch cubes
- ✧ 2 tablespoons olive oil
- ✧ 2 teaspoons fresh sage, finely chopped
- ✧ 1 teaspoon smoked paprika
- ✧ Salt and pepper, to taste
- ✧ Grated Parmigiano, for garnish
- ✧ Fresh sage leaves, for garnish

Air-Fried Butternut Squash with Sage

 10'   20'   4 Easy

Did you know that butternut squash is not just tasty but also rich in vitamins A and C, which are essential for immune health and skin vitality? Cooking it in the air fryer not only maintains these vital nutrients but also enhances its natural sweetness, making it a delightful side or main dish. For a twist, sprinkle a pinch of cinnamon before serving to add a warm, spicy note that complements the squash beautifully.

Directions

- ✧ Prepare Squash: In a large bowl, toss butternut squash cubes with olive oil, chopped sage, smoked paprika, salt, and pepper until well coated.
- ✧ Preheat Air Fryer: Set the air fryer to 380°F.
- ✧ Arrange Squash: Place the seasoned squash cubes in a single layer in the air fryer basket, avoiding overcrowding. Cook in batches if necessary.
- ✧ Cooking Process: Air fry for 20 minutes, shaking the basket halfway through, until the squash is golden and tender.
- ✧ Serve: Garnish the cooked squash with grated Parmigiano and fresh sage leaves before serving.

Nutritional values per serving - Calories: 120 Fat: 7 g Sodium: 100 mg Carbohydrates: 15 g Protein: 2 g

Ingredients

- 1 cup dried chickpeas, soaked overnight, drained
- 1/2 onion, roughly chopped
- 3 cloves garlic
- 1/2 cup fresh parsley
- 1/2 cup fresh cilantro
- 1 teaspoon ground cumin
- 1 teaspoon ground coriander
- 1/2 teaspoon paprika
- Salt and pepper, to taste
- Olive oil spray
- For the Tahini Sauce:
- 1/4 cup tahini
- 2 tablespoons lemon juice
- 2 tablespoons water
- 1 clove garlic, minced
- Salt, to taste

Air-Fried Falafel with Tahini Sauce

 20'*   15'   4   Easy

* plus overnight soaking

For an even more flavorful twist, add a pinch of sumac to the falafel mix for its tangy lemon-like zing. It's a delightful way to enhance the Mediterranean flair of the dish, embracing both the simplicity and the rich culinary heritage of the region.

Directions

- Blend Ingredients: In a food processor, blend soaked chickpeas, onion, garlic, parsley, cilantro, and spices until the mixture is coarse and grainy.
- Form Falafel: Shape the mixture into small balls or patties.
- Preheat Air Fryer: Set the air fryer to 360°F.
- Arrange in Basket: Spray the air fryer basket with olive oil and arrange falafel balls so they do not touch, ensuring even cooking.
- Cooking Process: Cook for 15 minutes, turning halfway, until the falafels are golden and crispy.
- Prepare Sauce: While falafels cook, whisk together all tahini sauce ingredients until smooth.
- Serve: Enjoy the hot falafels with tahini sauce drizzled over them or on the side for dipping.

Nutritional values per serving - Calories: 330 Fat: 12 g Sodium: 320 mg Carbohydrates: 42 g Protein: 13 g

Broccoli and Carrot Fritters

 15'   12'   4   Easy

Transforming vegetables into delightful fritters is a fantastic way to encourage kids and adults alike to enjoy their greens. For a gluten-free alternative, you can substitute all-purpose flour with chickpea flour, which not only adds a nutty flavor but also boosts protein content, making it a healthier choice without compromising on taste.

Ingredients

- 1 cup broccoli florets, finely chopped
- 1 cup carrots, grated
- 2 large eggs
- 1/2 cup all-purpose flour
- 1/2 teaspoon garlic powder
- 1/2 teaspoon paprika
- 1/4 cup chopped fresh parsley
- Salt and pepper, to taste
- Olive oil spray
- For garnish: Crumbled feta cheese and chopped spring onions

Directions

- Mix Ingredients: In a large bowl, mix broccoli, carrots, eggs, flour, and seasonings until well combined.
- Preheat Air Fryer: Set the air fryer to 360°F.
- Form Patties: Shape the vegetable mixture into small, 3-inch diameter patties.
- Arrange in Basket: Spray the air fryer basket with olive oil and place patties in a single layer without touching.
- Cook Patties: Cook for 6 minutes, flip, and continue cooking for another 6 minutes until golden and crispy.
- Serve: Present the patties hot, topped with crumbled feta cheese and chopped spring onions.

Nutritional values per serving - Calories: 155 Fat: 4 g Sodium: 120 mg Carbohydrates: 22 g Protein: 7 g

Cauliflower Steaks with Herb Dressing

 10' 20' 4 Easy

To give these cauliflower steaks a Sicilian twist, sprinkle some crushed capers and olives over the top before serving. The briny kick perfectly complements the mild cauliflower and vibrant herbs, transporting your taste buds straight to the Mediterranean coast.

Ingredients

- ✧ 2 large heads of cauliflower
- ✧ 2 tablespoons olive oil
- ✧ 1 teaspoon turmeric
- ✧ 1 teaspoon paprika
- ✧ Salt and pepper, to taste

For the Herb Dressing:

- ✧ 1/4 cup chopped fresh parsley
- ✧ 1/4 cup chopped fresh basil
- ✧ 2 tablespoons chopped fresh chives
- ✧ 1 clove garlic, minced
- ✧ 1/3 cup olive oil
- ✧ 2 tablespoons lemon juice
- ✧ Salt and pepper, to taste

Directions

- ✧ Prepare Cauliflower: Remove leaves, trim the stem, and slice the cauliflower into 1/2-inch thick steaks.
- ✧ Season Steaks: Brush each steak with olive oil and season with turmeric, paprika, salt, and pepper.
- ✧ Preheat Air Fryer: Set the air fryer to 380°F.
- ✧ Arrange in Basket: Place cauliflower steaks in the air fryer basket in a single layer, working in batches if needed.
- ✧ Cook Steaks: Cook for 10 minutes, flip, and continue cooking for another 10 minutes until golden and tender.
- ✧ Prepare Dressing: Whisk together all dressing ingredients in a small bowl during cooking.
- ✧ Serve: Drizzle herb dressing over the hot cauliflower steaks and serve.

Nutritional values per serving - Calories: 210 Fat: 18 g Sodium: 75 mg Carbohydrates: 11 g Protein: 3 g

Ingredients

- ✧ 1 can (15 oz) chickpeas, drained and rinsed
- ✧ 1 medium carrot, grated
- ✧ 1 zucchini, grated
- ✧ 1/2 red bell pepper, finely diced
- ✧ 2 cloves garlic, minced
- ✧ 1/4 cup chopped fresh parsley
- ✧ 2 tablespoons chopped fresh cilantro
- ✧ 1 teaspoon ground cumin
- ✧ 1 teaspoon smoked paprika
- ✧ 1/2 teaspoon coriander
- ✧ Salt and pepper, to taste
- ✧ 1/2 cup breadcrumbs
- ✧ 1 large egg, beaten

Chickpea and Vegetable Patties

 15' 20' 4 Easy

For a delightful twist, add a pinch of sumac to the patty mixture before cooking. This Middle Eastern spice will not only add a lemony zing but also a touch of exotic flavor, enhancing the overall taste profile of these nutritious patties.

Directions

- ✧ Blend Ingredients: In a food processor, combine chickpeas, garlic, spices, salt, and pepper. Pulse until coarsely ground.
- ✧ Mix Patty Mixture: Transfer to a large bowl, add carrot, zucchini, bell pepper, parsley, cilantro, breadcrumbs, and egg. Mix well.
- ✧ Form Patties: Shape the mixture into 8 patties, each about 1/2 inch thick.
- ✧ Preheat Air Fryer: Set the air fryer to 360°F.
- ✧ Arrange Patties: Spray the air fryer basket with non-stick spray, place patties in, avoiding overcrowding. Cook in batches if necessary.
- ✧ Cook Patties: Cook for 10 minutes, flip each patty, and continue for another 10 minutes until golden and crispy.
- ✧ Serve: Offer hot with dipping sauce or on a salad bed.

Nutritional values per serving - Calories: 240 Fat: 4 g Sodium: 300 mg Carbohydrates: 40 g Protein: 8 g

Ingredients

- 8 slices of halloumi cheese (about 1/2 inch thick)
- 1 zucchini, sliced into rounds
- 1 red bell pepper, sliced into strips
- 1 yellow bell pepper, sliced into strips
- 1 red onion, cut into wedges
- 2 tablespoons olive oil
- 1 teaspoon dried oregano
- 1/2 teaspoon smoked paprika
- Freshly ground black pepper, to taste
- A handful of fresh basil leaves, for garnish
- Lemon wedges, for serving

GRILLED HALLOUMI WITH VEGETABLES

 10' 15' 4 Easy

To enhance the Mediterranean flavors, drizzle a bit of balsamic glaze over the halloumi and vegetables before serving. This adds a sweet and tangy contrast that perfectly complements the salty cheese and savory veggies.

Directions

- Prepare Vegetables: In a large bowl, combine zucchini, bell peppers, and red onion with olive oil, oregano, smoked paprika, and black pepper. Toss well.
- Preheat Air Fryer: Set the air fryer to 375°F.
- Cook Vegetables: Place the seasoned vegetables in the air fryer basket. Cook for 10 minutes, shaking halfway through.
- Add Halloumi: Place halloumi slices over the vegetables. Continue cooking for 5 more minutes until the cheese is golden.
- Serve: Remove from air fryer, garnish with fresh basil, and serve with lemon wedges.

Nutritional values per serving - Calories: 320 Fat: 24 g Sodium: 870 mg Carbohydrates: 10 g Protein: 18 g

GRILLED PORTOBELLO MUSHROOMS

 10' 8' 4 Easy

Portobello mushrooms are like nature's steak for vegetarians due to their meaty texture. For an extra zing, try adding a splash of balsamic vinegar before serving. It enhances the earthy flavors beautifully!

Ingredients

- 4 large portobello mushroom caps, stems removed
- 2 tablespoons olive oil
- 2 cloves garlic, minced
- 1 teaspoon fresh rosemary, finely chopped
- 1 teaspoon fresh thyme, finely chopped
- Salt and freshly ground black pepper, to taste
- 1/4 cup grated Parmigiano cheese
- Fresh parsley, chopped for garnish

Directions

- Prepare Mushrooms: Clean the mushroom caps with a damp cloth and remove the gills if desired.
- Season: In a small bowl, combine olive oil, garlic, rosemary, and thyme. Brush the mixture over both sides of the mushroom caps and season with salt and pepper.
- Preheat Air Fryer: Set the air fryer to 375°F.
- Cook Mushrooms: Place the mushroom caps, gill side up, in the air fryer basket. Cook for 8 minutes until tender.
- Add Cheese: Sprinkle Parmigiano over the mushrooms in the last minute of cooking to melt.
- Serve: Garnish with chopped parsley and serve.

Nutritional values per serving - Calories: 150 Fat: 11 g Sodium: 200 mg Carbohydrates: 6 g Protein: 6 g

Mediterranean Stuffed Zucchini

 15'   20'   4 Easy

Zucchini is a wonderfully versatile vegetable that beautifully absorbs flavors from herbs and spices. For a lovely variation, add a pinch of sumac before serving for a tangy twist that complements the feta cheese splendidly!

Ingredients

- 4 medium zucchini, halved lengthwise
- 1 tablespoon olive oil
- 1 small onion, finely chopped
- 2 cloves garlic, minced
- 1 red bell pepper, diced
- 1/2 cup cooked quinoa (Ch. 8)
- 1/2 cup crumbled feta cheese
- 1/4 cup chopped kalamata olives
- 1 tablespoon chopped fresh parsley
- 1 tablespoon chopped fresh basil
- Salt and freshly ground black pepper, to taste
- 2 tablespoons grated Parmigiano, for topping

Directions

- Prepare Zucchini: Hollow out each zucchini half to a 1/4-inch thick shell. Chop the removed flesh and set aside.
- Sauté Vegetables: In a skillet with heated olive oil, sauté onion, garlic, bell pepper, and reserved zucchini flesh until soft, about 8 minutes.
- Mix Filling: Off heat, combine the sautéed mixture with cooked quinoa, feta, olives, parsley, and basil. Season with salt and pepper.
- Stuff Zucchini: Fill the zucchini shells with the mixture, pressing it in firmly.
- Preheat and Cook: Set the air fryer to 360°F and place the stuffed zucchini in the basket. Cook for 15-20 minutes until tender.
- Add Cheese: Top with Parmigiano during the last 2 minutes of cooking.
- Serve: Present the zucchini warm.

Nutritional values per serving - Calories: 180 Fat: 11 g Sodium: 320 mg Carbohydrates: 15 g Protein: 8 g

Ingredients

- 1 lb. asparagus, ends trimmed
- 2 tablespoons olive oil
- 1/2 cup grated Parmigiano cheese
- 1/4 cup breadcrumbs
- 1 teaspoon garlic powder
- 1/2 teaspoon paprika
- Salt and freshly ground black pepper, to taste
- Lemon wedges, for serving

Parmesan-Crusted Asparagus

 10'   8'   4 Easy

For a delightful twist on this classic dish, try adding a sprinkle of chopped fresh herbs such as rosemary or thyme before serving. Not only will this enhance the flavor, but it will also add a pop of color and freshness that makes the dish even more appealing!

Directions

- Coat Asparagus: In a large bowl, toss the asparagus with olive oil.
- Prepare Coating: Mix Parmigiano, breadcrumbs, garlic powder, paprika, salt, and pepper in a separate bowl.
- Dredge Asparagus: Roll each asparagus spear in the Parmigiano mixture until fully coated.
- Preheat Air Fryer: Set the air fryer to 400°F.
- Arrange in Basket: Place asparagus in a single layer in the basket, avoiding overcrowding. Cook in batches if needed.
- Cook: Air fry for 7-8 minutes until asparagus is tender and coating is golden.
- Serve: Offer immediately with lemon wedges for added zest.

Nutritional values per serving - Calories: 150 Fat: 10 g Sodium: 250 mg Carbohydrates: 10 g Protein: 8 g

Ingredients

- 4 large bell peppers, tops cut off and seeds removed
- 1 cup cooked quinoa (Ch. 8)
- 1 can (15 oz) black beans, drained and rinsed
- 1 cup corn kernels (fresh, canned, or thawed from frozen)
- 1/2 cup diced tomatoes
- 1/2 cup crumbled feta cheese
- 1/4 cup finely chopped red onion
- 1/4 cup chopped fresh cilantro
- 1 teaspoon cumin
- 1/2 teaspoon paprika
- Salt and pepper, to taste
- Olive oil, for drizzling
- Additional crumbled feta cheese and fresh cilantro, for garnish

QUINOA-STUFFED BELL PEPPERS

 15'   20'   4 Easy

To bring a unique twist to this dish, try incorporating a pinch of sumac into the stuffing mix before cooking. Sumac not only adds a beautiful tangy flavor that complements the sweetness of the bell peppers but also introduces a splash of color, making this dish as delightful to look at as it is to eat.

Directions

- Mix Filling: In a large bowl, combine quinoa, black beans, corn, tomatoes, feta, onion, cilantro, cumin, paprika, salt, and pepper.
- Stuff Peppers: Evenly distribute the mixture into the hollowed-out bell peppers.
- Prepare for Cooking: Drizzle olive oil over the peppers and place them upright in the air fryer basket.
- Cook: Set the air fryer to 350°F and cook for 15-20 minutes until peppers are tender.
- Serve: Garnish with more feta and fresh cilantro before serving.

Nutritional values per serving - Calories: 250 Fat: 7 g Sodium: 400 mg Carbohydrates: 38 g Protein: 10 g

SPINACH AND FETA STUFFED MUSHROOMS

 10'   15'   4   Easy

For an extra touch of Italian flair, try adding a sprinkle of grated Parmigiano over the stuffed mushrooms before air frying. This not only enhances the flavors but also creates a beautifully crispy top that complements the creamy filling.

Ingredients

- 16 large button mushrooms, stems removed and finely chopped, caps reserved
- 2 tablespoons olive oil
- 2 cloves garlic, minced
- 1 cup fresh spinach, chopped
- 1/2 cup crumbled feta cheese
- 1/4 cup breadcrumbs
- 2 tablespoons fresh parsley, chopped
- 1 tablespoon fresh dill, chopped
- Salt and pepper, to taste
- 1/4 teaspoon crushed red pepper flakes (optional)
- Additional chopped parsley or dill. for garnish

Directions

- Preheat Air Fryer: Set to 350°F.
- Sauté Fillings: In a skillet with olive oil, sauté mushroom stems and garlic until soft, about 5 minutes. Add spinach and cook until wilted, 2 minutes.
- Prepare Filling: Let the sautéed mixture cool, then combine with feta, breadcrumbs, parsley, dill, and seasonings in a bowl.
- Stuff Mushrooms: Fill each mushroom cap with the mixture, pressing firmly.
- Cook: Brush stuffed mushrooms with olive oil, place in the air fryer, and cook for 10-15 minutes until tender and golden.
- Garnish and Serve: Sprinkle with parsley or dill before serving.

Nutritional values per serving - Calories: 150 Fat: 10 g Sodium: 300 mg Carbohydrates: 9 g Protein: 6 g

Spinach and Ricotta Stuffed Peppers

 15' 20' 4 Easy

If you want to add a touch of zest, sprinkle some crushed red pepper flakes into the ricotta mixture before stuffing the peppers. It gives a lovely warmth that cuts through the creamy richness of the ricotta!

Ingredients

- 4 bell peppers, tops cut off and seeds removed
- 1 tablespoon olive oil
- 1 small onion, finely chopped
- 2 cloves garlic, minced
- 2 cups fresh spinach, roughly chopped
- 1 cup ricotta cheese
- 1/2 cup grated Parmigiano cheese
- 1/4 cup breadcrumbs
- 1 teaspoon dried oregano
- Salt and black pepper to taste
- Fresh basil leaves, for garnish

Directions

- Preheat Air Fryer: Set to 375°F.
- Sauté Vegetables: Heat olive oil in a skillet, then sauté onion and garlic until softened, about 3-4 minutes.
- Cook Spinach: Add spinach and cook until wilted, about 2 minutes. Remove from heat and cool slightly.
- Prepare Filling: In a bowl, mix the cooled spinach with ricotta, Parmigiano, breadcrumbs, oregano, salt, and pepper.
- Stuff Peppers: Fill each pepper with the spinach mixture.
- Arrange in Basket: Place peppers upright in the air fryer basket.
- Cook: Air fry for 15-20 minutes until peppers are tender and filling is golden.
- Garnish and Serve: Top with fresh basil before serving.

Nutritional values per serving - Calories: 220 Fat: 14 g Sodium: 340 mg Carbohydrates: 16 g Protein: 12 g

Ingredients

- 2 large eggplants, halved lengthwise
- 2 tablespoons olive oil
- 1 medium onion, diced
- 2 cloves garlic, minced
- 1 cup chopped tomatoes
- 1/2 cup cooked quinoa (Ch. 8)
- 1/4 cup chopped fresh parsley
- 1/4 cup chopped fresh basil
- 1/2 cup crumbled feta cheese
- Salt and pepper, to taste
- 2 tablespoons pine nuts (optional, for garnish)
- Additional chopped parsley and basil for garnish

Stuffed Eggplant

 20' 25' 4 Easy

A delightful twist to this dish is to drizzle a bit of balsamic glaze over the top before serving. It adds a sweet and tangy pop that beautifully complements the creamy feta and hearty eggplant!

Directions

- Preheat Air Fryer: Set the air fryer to 360°F.
- Prepare Eggplants: Scoop out the flesh of the eggplants, leaving a 1/2-inch border. Chop the scooped flesh.
- Sauté Aromatics: Heat olive oil in a skillet and sauté onion and garlic until translucent.
- Cook Eggplant Flesh: Add the chopped eggplant flesh to the skillet and cook until softened.
- Add Remaining Ingredients: Stir in tomatoes, quinoa, parsley, and basil. Cook until combined. Season with salt and pepper.
- Stuff Eggplants: Fill the eggplant shells with the mixture and top with crumbled feta.
- Oil and Cook: Brush the outer skins with olive oil. Place stuffed eggplants in the air fryer basket.
- Air Fry: Cook for 20-25 minutes until the eggplants are tender and golden on top.
- Garnish and Serve: Finish with pine nuts, parsley, and basil.

Nutritional values per serving - Calories: 290 Fat: 18 g Sodium: 320 mg Carbohydrates: 27 g Protein: 9 g

Ingredients

- 4 large bell peppers (assorted colors)
- 1 tablespoon olive oil
- 1 onion, finely chopped
- 2 cloves garlic, minced
- 1 cup cooked rice (brown or white)
- 1 can (15 oz) black beans, drained and rinsed
- 1 teaspoon ground cumin
- 1 teaspoon paprika
- 1/2 teaspoon ground coriander
- Salt and pepper to taste
- 1/2 cup corn kernels (fresh or frozen)
- 1/2 cup vegan cheese, shredded
- Fresh cilantro, chopped for garnish

Stuffed Peppers with Vegan Cheese

 15' 20' 4 Easy

For a delightful twist, try adding a sprinkle of smoked paprika on top of the vegan cheese before air frying. It adds a lovely smoky flavor that complements the sweetness of the bell peppers and the savoriness of the filling!

Directions

- Preheat Air Fryer: Set to 380°F.
- Prepare Peppers: Remove tops, seeds, and membranes from bell peppers.
- Sauté Onion and Garlic: Heat olive oil in a skillet, then sauté onion and garlic until translucent.
- Mix Filling: Add rice, black beans, spices, and cook until heated. Off heat, mix in corn.
- Stuff Peppers: Fill peppers with the rice and bean mixture, topping with vegan cheese.
- Cook in Air Fryer: Place stuffed peppers in basket, cooking until tender and cheese melts.
- Garnish and Serve: Finish with chopped cilantro.

Nutritional values per serving - Calories: 265 Fat: 7 g Sodium: 480 mg Carbohydrates: 42 g Protein: 9 g

Tofu with Mediterranean Spices

 10' 15' 4 Easy

A wonderful variation to this dish is to add a pinch of chili flakes for a spicy kick, or sprinkle some crumbled feta cheese on top just before serving for a creamy contrast. Tofu absorbs flavors beautifully, making it a versatile canvas for the vibrant spices of the Mediterranean!

Ingredients

- 1 block (14 oz) firm tofu, pressed and cut into 1-inch cubes
- 2 tablespoons olive oil
- 1 teaspoon turmeric
- 1 teaspoon paprika
- 1/2 teaspoon ground cumin
- 1/2 teaspoon coriander
- 1/4 teaspoon sumac
- Salt and black pepper to taste
- Fresh parsley, chopped for garnish
- Lemon wedges, for serving

Directions

- Prepare Spice Mix: In a bowl, combine olive oil, turmeric, paprika, cumin, coriander, sumac, salt, and pepper.
- Coat Tofu: Add tofu cubes to the spice mix and toss gently to coat.
- Preheat Air Fryer: Set to 375°F.
- Arrange Tofu: Place tofu cubes in a single layer in the air fryer basket, avoiding overcrowding.
- Cook Tofu: Air fry for 15 minutes, shaking the basket halfway through until golden and crispy.
- Garnish and Serve: Top with fresh parsley and accompany with lemon wedges.

Nutritional values per serving - Calories: 150 Fat: 10 g Sodium: 200 mg Carbohydrates: 3 g Protein: 10 g

Vegan Meatballs

 15' 20' 4 Easy

For a delightful twist, add a pinch of crushed red pepper flakes to the meatball mix for a gentle heat that dances on the palate. These vegan meatballs can also be served in a rich tomato basil sauce over freshly cooked pasta for a comforting meal.

Ingredients

- 1 cup cooked chickpeas, drained and rinsed
- 1/2 cup breadcrumbs
- 1/4 cup nutritional yeast
- 1/4 cup chopped fresh parsley
- 2 cloves garlic, minced
- 1 tablespoon soy sauce
- 1 teaspoon smoked paprika
- 1/2 teaspoon ground cumin
- 1/2 teaspoon dried oregano
- Salt and black pepper to taste
- Olive oil spray

Directions

- Prepare Meatball Mix: In a food processor, blend chickpeas, breadcrumbs, nutritional yeast, parsley, garlic, soy sauce, smoked paprika, cumin, oregano, salt, and pepper until combined but textured.
- Form Meatballs: Scoop out and roll the mixture into tablespoon-sized balls.
- Preheat Air Fryer: Set to 375°F.
- Arrange Meatballs: Spray the air fryer basket with olive oil and place meatballs inside, ensuring they don't touch.
- Cook Meatballs: Air fry for 20 minutes, shaking the basket after 10 minutes, until golden and firm.
- Serve: Enjoy hot with your preferred dipping sauce or alongside pasta.

Nutritional values per serving - Calories: 180 Fat: 4 g Sodium: 400 mg Carbohydrates: 27 g Protein: 8 g

Ingredients

- 1 cup mashed potatoes
- 1/2 cup cooked peas
- 1/2 cup finely chopped carrots
- 1/4 cup finely chopped onion
- 2 cloves garlic, minced
- 1 teaspoon grated ginger
- 1 teaspoon ground cumin
- 1 teaspoon coriander powder
- 1/2 teaspoon turmeric
- 1/4 teaspoon garam masala
- Salt and pepper to taste
- 8 spring roll wrappers
- Olive oil spray

Veggie Samosas

 20' 15' 4 Easy

To add a delightful twist, sprinkle a pinch of smoked paprika over the samosas before air frying. This will give them a unique smoky flavor that complements the spices beautifully. Remember, samosas are not just a dish; they are a piece of culinary art that brings joy to the table!

Directions

- Prepare Filling: In a large bowl, mix mashed potatoes, peas, carrots, onion, garlic, ginger, cumin, coriander, turmeric, garam masala, salt, and pepper thoroughly.
- Wrap Samosas: Place about 2 tablespoons of filling on one corner of a spring roll wrapper. Fold into a triangle, continuing to fold until the wrapper is fully wrapped. Seal edges with water.
- Preheat Air Fryer: Set to 360°F.
- Arrange Samosas: Spray the air fryer basket with olive oil and place samosas without overlapping. Spray the tops of the samosas with additional oil.
- Cook: Air fry for 8 minutes, flip, and continue for another 7 minutes until golden and crispy.
- Serve: Enjoy hot with mint chutney (Ch. 8) or tamarind sauce.

Nutritional values per serving - Calories: 210 Fat: 4 g Sodium: 320 mg Carbohydrates: 35 g Protein: 5 g

Chapter 7. Desserts

Desserts always mark the sweet climax of our gatherings, bringing smiles all around. As a retired Italian chef with undiminished zeal for cooking, I'm thrilled to guide you through crafting desserts with your air fryer—turning classic treats into modern marvels with less oil and flawless results. Whether it's crispy cookies or soft cakes, your air fryer proves astonishingly adept.

A meal without a dessert is like a day without sunshine, and true to that saying, we'll explore adapting beloved Mediterranean and American desserts for air frying. These recipes are designed to be simple, enabling even novices to dazzle with delicious desserts, each accompanied by tips for personal touches, like a dash of cinnamon or a zest of lemon to transform the simple into the sublime.

Join me in warming up the air fryer for a journey of culinary delight, blending innovation with ease. Let these recipes reflect the enchantment of air frying, mingling warmth, flavor, and texture. Together, we'll venture through each recipe, enriched with anecdotes from my Italian heritage and culinary experiences. Here's to desserts that comfort, enchant, and bring a slice of Italy to your table. *Buon appetito!*

Air-Fried Churros

 20'   10'   4   Easy

In Spain, where churros are a beloved treat, they're often enjoyed with a cup of thick, hot chocolate. Making them in the air fryer not only reduces the mess and calories but also keeps the outside wonderfully crisp. A little tip for an extra touch of delight: add a pinch of chili powder to the sugar coating for a subtle warmth that dances on the palate.

Ingredients

- 1 cup water
- 2 1/2 tablespoons granulated sugar
- 1/2 teaspoon salt
- 2 tablespoons vegetable oil
- 1 cup all-purpose flour
- 1 teaspoon vanilla extract
- 1/4 teaspoon ground cinnamon (optional)

Directions

- Prepare the Dough: In a medium saucepan, combine water, sugar, salt, and vegetable oil. Bring to a boil over medium heat. Remove from heat and stir in the flour until well blended. Mix in vanilla and optional cinnamon until the dough forms a ball.
- Rest the Dough: Allow the dough to rest for 10 minutes. This makes it easier to handle.
- Preheat Air Fryer: Set the air fryer to 375°F and let it warm up while you prepare the churros.
- Pipe the Churros: Transfer the dough to a piping bag fitted with a large star tip. Pipe the dough into 4-inch strips directly into the air fryer basket, leaving space between each for expansion.
- Cook: Air fry the churros for about 10 minutes or until golden brown and crisp.
- Prepare the Coating: Mix sugar and cinnamon in a shallow dish. Toss the warm churros in the sugar mixture until well coated.
- Serve: Serve warm with a side of chocolate sauce (Ch. 8) or dulce de leche for dipping.

Nutritional values per serving - Calories: 220 Fat: 8 g Sodium: 300 mg Carbohydrates: 34 g Protein: 3 g

Apple Cinnamon Chips

 10'   20'   4   Easy

In my hometown, apple chips were a cherished autumn treat. For an extra layer of flavor, try adding a sprinkle of vanilla powder or a drizzle of honey before cooking. This not only enhances the sweetness but also brings a comforting warmth to this simple, healthy snack. Remember, the key to perfect apple chips in the air fryer is thin, even slices — patience here pays off with every crispy bite!

Ingredients

- 4 large apples (any sweet variety like Fuji or Honeycrisp)
- 1 teaspoon ground cinnamon
- 1/4 teaspoon nutmeg (optional)
- A pinch of ground cloves (optional)
- Cooking spray or 1 tablespoon melted coconut oil

Directions

- Prep the Apples: Wash and thinly slice the apples. Remove the seeds and core. The thinner the slices, the crispier the chips will be.
- Season: In a large bowl, toss the apple slices with cinnamon, nutmeg, and cloves until evenly coated. If using, drizzle with coconut oil for extra crispness.
- Arrange: Spray the air fryer basket with cooking spray. Lay the apple slices in a single layer in the basket, ensuring they do not overlap. You may need to work in batches depending on the size of your air fryer.
- Air Fry: Cook at 300°F for about 15 minutes or until the apple slices are crispy and golden. Halfway through, flip the slices to ensure even cooking.
- Cool: Let the chips cool in the basket for a few minutes to crisp up further before serving.

Nutritional values per serving - Calories: 95 Fat: 2 g Sodium: 50 mg Carbohydrates: 25 g Protein: 1 g

Apple Fritters

 15'   10'   4 Easy

Ingredients

- 2 large apples, peeled, cored, and diced
- 1 cup all-purpose flour
- 1/4 cup granulated sugar
- 1 teaspoon baking powder
- 1/2 teaspoon ground cinnamon
- 1/4 teaspoon nutmeg
- Pinch of salt
- 1/3 cup milk
- 1 large egg
- 1 teaspoon vanilla extract
- Powdered sugar for dusting

Apple fritters remind me of the vibrant autumn festivals in Italy, where the air is as crisp as the apples. For a twist, try adding a splash of rum to the batter before cooking, or a pinch of clove for a deeper spice note. Each bite will transport you to those joyous moments under the golden leaves. And remember, using the air fryer instead of deep-frying not only saves calories but also helps maintain a cleaner kitchen!

Directions

- Combine Dry Ingredients: In a large mixing bowl, whisk together flour, granulated sugar, baking powder, cinnamon, nutmeg, and salt.
- Mix Wet Ingredients: In another bowl, beat the egg, milk, and vanilla extract until well combined.
- Form Batter: Pour the wet ingredients into the dry ingredients and stir until just combined. Fold in the diced apples until they are evenly coated with the batter.
- Preheat Air Fryer: Preheat the air fryer to 350°F for about 3 minutes.
- Cook the Fritters: Spoon mounds of the batter into the air fryer basket, spaced apart. Work in batches if needed. Cook for 10 minutes, flipping halfway through, or until the fritters are golden and cooked through.
- Serve: Dust the warm fritters with powdered sugar and serve immediately for the best texture.

Nutritional values per serving - Calories: 240 Fat: 3 g Sodium: 150 mg Carbohydrates: 50 g Protein: 4 g

Ingredients

- 10 sheets of phyllo dough, cut in half
- 1 cup finely chopped walnuts
- 1/2 cup finely chopped pistachios
- 1/4 cup sugar
- 1 teaspoon ground cinnamon
- 1/2 teaspoon ground cardamom
- 1/4 cup melted butter

For the Syrup:

- 1/2 cup water
- 1 cup sugar
- 1 tablespoon lemon juice
- 1/2 teaspoon rose water (optional)

BAKLAVA ROLLS

 20' 15' 4 Medium

Did you know? Baklava is believed to have been perfected in the imperial kitchens of Topkapi Palace in Istanbul, making it a treat fit for sultans and kings! When preparing baklava, always keep the phyllo dough covered with a damp cloth to prevent it from drying out. It's little attentions like this that turn simple ingredients into royal delights!

Directions

- Prepare the Filling: Mix the walnuts, pistachios, sugar, cinnamon, and cardamom in a bowl.
- Assemble the Rolls: Lay a sheet of phyllo on a flat surface, brush lightly with melted butter, place about 2 tablespoons of the nut mixture at one end, and roll up tightly. Repeat with remaining phyllo sheets.
- Preheat the Air Fryer: Set the air fryer to 350°F.
- Cook the Baklava Rolls: Place the rolls in the air fryer basket, ensuring they do not touch. Air fry for 12-15 minutes or until golden and crisp.
- Make the Syrup: While the baklava cooks, combine water, sugar, and lemon juice in a small saucepan. Bring to a boil, then simmer for about 10 minutes. Stir in rose water if using.
- Finish the Baklava: Drizzle the hot syrup over the hot baklava rolls immediately after removing them from the air fryer.
- Let Cool: Allow to cool for a few minutes before serving to let the syrup soak in.

Nutritional values per serving - Calories: 480 Fat: 24 g Sodium: 300 mg Carbohydrates: 62 g Protein: 8 g

BANANA BREAD

 10' 40' 4 Easy

Bananas are not just delicious; they're also rich in potassium and fiber, making this banana bread not only a treat for your taste buds but also good for your heart. For a twist, try adding a handful of chopped walnuts or chocolate chips for that extra special touch that turns a simple recipe into a family favorite.

Ingredients

- 3 ripe bananas, mashed
- 1/3 cup melted butter
- 1 teaspoon baking soda
- Pinch of salt
- 3/4 cup sugar
- 1 large egg, beaten
- 1 teaspoon vanilla extract
- 1/2 teaspoon cinnamon
- 1/4 teaspoon nutmeg
- 1 1/2 cups of all-purpose flour

Directions

- Prep the Ingredients: In a mixing bowl, stir together the mashed bananas and melted butter.
- Mix Dry Ingredients: In a separate bowl, combine baking soda, salt, sugar, cinnamon, nutmeg, and flour.
- Combine Mixtures: Stir the dry ingredients into the banana mixture, then add the beaten egg and vanilla extract. Mix until well combined.
- Prepare for Air Frying: Grease a cake pan that fits your air fryer basket. Pour the batter into the pan.
- Air Frying: Preheat the air fryer to 320°F. Place the pan in the air fryer basket and cook for about 40 minutes, or until a toothpick inserted into the center comes out clean.
- Cooling: Allow the banana bread to cool in the pan for 10 minutes before removing.

Nutritional values per serving - Calories: 330 Fat: 10 g Sodium: 250 mg Carbohydrates: 56 g Protein: 4 g

Chocolate Stuffed Croissants

 10' 8' 4 Easy

In Italy, we say that even a simple meal can bring joy if made with love. These croissants are a perfect example—simple, yet luxurious. If you're feeling adventurous, sprinkle a little orange zest or a dash of cinnamon into the chocolate before rolling up the croissants for a citrusy twist or a warm spice note that dances on the palate.

Ingredients

✧ 1 package refrigerated croissant dough (8 count)
✧ 8 pieces of dark chocolate or 1/2 cup chocolate chips
✧ 1 egg, beaten (for egg wash)
✧ Powdered sugar for dusting (optional)

Directions

✧ Prepare the Dough: Unroll the croissant dough and separate it into triangles along the perforations.
✧ Add Chocolate: Place a piece of chocolate or a tablespoon of chocolate chips at the wider end of each triangle.
✧ Roll and Seal: Roll the dough up starting from the chocolate-stuffed end towards the small tip to form a croissant shape. Make sure the edges are sealed to keep the chocolate from leaking.
✧ Egg Wash: Lightly brush each croissant with the beaten egg for a golden finish.
✧ Air Frying: Preheat the air fryer to 350°F. Place the croissants in the air fryer basket, ensuring they are not touching. Cook for 8 minutes, or until they are golden brown and puffed up.
✧ Serving: Let them cool slightly and dust with powdered sugar before serving, if desired.

Nutritional values per serving - Calories: 290 Fat: 16 g Sodium: 380 mg Carbohydrates: 34 g Protein: 5 g

Ingredients

✧ 1 cup all-purpose flour
✧ 1/4 cup granulated sugar
✧ 1 teaspoon baking powder
✧ 1/2 teaspoon ground cinnamon
✧ 1/4 teaspoon nutmeg
✧ 1/4 teaspoon salt

✧ 1/4 cup milk
✧ 1 large egg
✧ 2 tablespoons unsalted butter, melted
✧ 1 teaspoon vanilla extract

For Coating:

✧ 1/4 cup granulated sugar
✧ 1 teaspoon ground cinnamon

Cinnamon Sugar Donut Holes

 15' 10' 4* Easy

* serves about 16 donut holes

Making donut holes in the air fryer not only reduces the mess and calories from deep frying but also keeps the kitchen cooler. For a festive twist during the holidays, mix a bit of ground cardamom into your cinnamon sugar. It's my little secret to making these simple treats feel extra special!

Directions

✧ Prepare the Batter: In a mixing bowl, combine flour, 1/4 cup sugar, baking powder, 1/2 teaspoon cinnamon, nutmeg, and salt. In another bowl, whisk together the milk, egg, melted butter, and vanilla. Add the wet ingredients to the dry ingredients, stirring until just combined.
✧ Shape the Donut Holes: Using your hands or a small ice cream scoop, form the dough into small balls about the size of a walnut.
✧ Air Fry: Preheat the air fryer to 350°F. Place the dough balls in the basket, making sure they do not touch. Cook for 10 minutes, turning halfway through until they are golden brown and cooked through.
✧ Cinnamon Sugar Coating: While the donut holes are cooking, mix 1/4 cup sugar with 1 teaspoon cinnamon in a shallow dish. Immediately toss the hot donut holes in the cinnamon sugar until well coated.
✧ Serve: Enjoy warm for the best flavor and texture.

Nutritional values per serving - Calories: 210 Fat: 5 g Sodium: 150 mg Carbohydrates: 37 g Protein: 4 g

Ingredients

- 6 sheets phyllo dough, thawed
- 1/4 cup unsalted butter, melted
- 1/2 cup finely chopped pistachios
- 1/4 cup honey, plus extra for drizzling
- 1 teaspoon ground cinnamon
- 1/4 teaspoon nutmeg
- Powdered sugar, for dusting

Honey and Pistachio Phyllo Bites

 20'   8'   4*   Easy

* makes about 12 bites

While phyllo dough isn't traditionally Italian—it hails from Greece and Turkey—these honey and pistachio bites pair wonderfully with our espresso tradition. Drizzling honey over the warm bites enhances the nuttiness of the pistachios, making these little desserts a perfect way to round off any meal. Enjoy them with a robust espresso to embrace the joy of simple, cross-cultural pleasures!

Directions

- Prepare Phyllo Sheets: Preheat your air fryer to 350°F. Lay one sheet of phyllo dough on a clean surface and brush lightly with melted butter. Stack another sheet on top, brush with butter, and repeat with a third sheet. Cut the layered sheets into four squares.
- Fill the Phyllo: Mix the chopped pistachios with honey, cinnamon, and nutmeg. Place a tablespoon of the pistachio mixture in the center of each phyllo square. Carefully gather the edges of the phyllo and pinch to form a small purse or bite, ensuring the filling is well enclosed.
- Air Fry: Place the phyllo bites in the air fryer basket, ensuring they do not touch. Cook for 6-8 minutes, or until golden and crisp.
- Serve: Dust the warm phyllo bites with powdered sugar and drizzle with a little more honey before serving.

Nutritional values per serving - Calories: 230 Fat: 12 g Sodium: 100 mg Carbohydrates: 28 g Protein: 4 g

Honey Roasted Peaches

 10'   5'   4   Easy

Roasting peaches in the air fryer intensifies their natural sweetness and makes the kitchen smell like heaven! Pair them with a scoop of vanilla gelato or a dollop of whipped cream for a simple yet elegant dessert. For a unique twist, a drizzle of balsamic reduction adds a lovely depth of flavor, merging traditional and modern tastes beautifully.

Ingredients

- 4 ripe peaches, halved and pitted
- 4 tablespoons honey
- 1/2 teaspoon ground cinnamon
- A pinch of nutmeg
- 1/2 teaspoon vanilla extract
- Fresh mint leaves, for garnish
- Optional: Crushed almonds or walnuts for topping

Directions

- Preheat Air Fryer: Set the air fryer to 375°F.
- Mix Ingredients: In a small bowl, combine the honey, cinnamon, nutmeg, and vanilla extract.
- Prepare Peaches: Brush the cut sides of the peaches with the honey mixture.
- Arrange in Basket: Place the peach halves, cut side up, in the air fryer basket without overlapping.
- Air Fry: Cook for 12-15 minutes until the peaches are tender and caramelized.
- Serve and Garnish: Top with fresh mint leaves and optional crushed nuts.

Nutritional values per serving - Calories: 120 Fat: 1 g Sodium: 50 mg Carbohydrates: 30 g Protein: 1 g

Lemon Ricotta Fritters

 15' 10' 4 Easy

These little lemon ricotta fritters are a nod to my childhood in Italy, where we celebrated simple pleasures. The air fryer gives them a delightful lightness without the oil of traditional frying. For an extra layer of flavor, try adding a sprinkle of cinnamon to the batter, or serve with a dollop of lemon curd! (Ch. 8)

Ingredients

- 1 cup ricotta cheese
- 1 large egg
- Zest of 1 lemon
- 2 tablespoons granulated sugar
- 1 teaspoon vanilla extract
- 3/4 cup all-purpose flour
- 1 teaspoon baking powder
- A pinch of salt
- Powdered sugar, for dusting
- Optional: Fresh berries for serving

Directions

- Mix Ingredients: In a large bowl, combine the ricotta, egg, lemon zest, sugar, and vanilla extract. Mix until well blended.
- Add Dry Ingredients: Sift in the flour, baking powder, and salt. Stir until just combined; do not overmix.
- Preheat Air Fryer: Set the air fryer to 350°F and lightly grease the basket with cooking spray.
- Form Fritters: Using a spoon, drop tablespoon-sized balls of the batter into the basket, making sure they do not touch.
- Cook: Air fry for 8-10 minutes or until they are golden brown and cooked through.
- Serve: Dust with powdered sugar and serve hot with optional fresh berries.

Nutritional values per serving - Calories: 180 Fat: 5 g Sodium: 180 mg Carbohydrates: 24 g Protein: 8 g

Mini Chocolate Hazelnut Pastries

 15' 8' 4 Easy

In Italy, we cherish our moments with *dolci* as a way to wrap up meals or sweeten our afternoon coffee. These pastries, inspired by my grandmother's love for anything with hazelnut, are perfect with an espresso. Feel free to substitute the hazelnut spread with any other nut butter for a twist on this classic treat!

Ingredients

- 1 package (1 lb.) pre-made puff pastry, thawed
- 1/2 cup chocolate hazelnut spread
- 1 egg, beaten for egg wash
- Optional: Powdered sugar for dusting

Directions

- Prep Pastry: Roll out the puff pastry on a lightly floured surface. Cut into 3-inch squares.
- Add Filling: Place a teaspoon of chocolate hazelnut spread in the center of each square.
- Form Pastries: Fold the corners of each square towards the center, lightly pressing to seal the edges. Brush with egg wash.
- Air Fry: Preheat the air fryer to 350°F. Place the pastries in the basket, not touching, and air fry for 8 minutes or until golden and puffed.
- Serve: Let cool slightly and dust with powdered sugar before serving.

Nutritional values per serving - Calories: 300 Fat: 18 g Sodium: 250 mg Carbohydrates: 30 g Protein: 4 g

Ingredients

- 2 large bananas, peeled and cut into 1/2-inch slices
- 1/4 cup creamy peanut butter
- 1/2 cup crushed nuts (e.g., almonds, pecans)
- Optional: Drizzle of honey or melted dark chocolate for topping

Peanut Butter Banana Bites

 10'   6'   4  Easy

While peanut butter isn't traditional in Italian kitchens, I've grown fond of its rich, creamy texture, especially paired with bananas. For a touch of Italian flair, sprinkle a bit of crushed amaretti cookies instead of nuts, merging the New World with Old World charm perfectly.

Directions

- Prepare Banana Slices: Arrange banana slices on a plate.
- Add Peanut Butter: Spread a small amount of peanut butter on top of each banana slice.
- Coat with Nuts: Press the peanut butter side of each banana slice into the crushed nuts to coat.
- Air Fry: Preheat the air fryer to 360°F. Place banana bites in the air fryer basket, nut side up, ensuring they do not touch. Air fry for 6 minutes or until the nuts are toasted.
- Serve: Drizzle with honey or melted chocolate if desired, and serve warm.

Nutritional values per serving - Calories: 210 Fat: 12 g
Sodium: 75 mg Carbohydrates: 24 g Protein: 4 g

Raspberry Crumble

 10'   15' 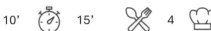 4   Easy

Raspberries remind me of the lush berry bushes back in Italy, although we are more used to seeing them in wild forests than in our kitchens! Pairing them with a traditional crumble topping brings a bit of Britain into our Italian-inspired air-fry feast. For a little twist, add a pinch of nutmeg to the crumble mix—it marries beautifully with the tartness of the berries.

Ingredients

- 2 cups fresh raspberries
- 1/4 cup granulated sugar
- 1 teaspoon vanilla extract
- 1/2 cup all-purpose flour
- 1/4 cup rolled oats
- 1/4 cup light brown sugar
- 1/4 teaspoon ground cinnamon
- 1/4 cup cold unsalted butter, diced
- Optional: Whipped cream or vanilla ice cream for serving

Directions

- Mix Filling: In a bowl, combine raspberries, granulated sugar, and vanilla extract. Gently toss to coat the raspberries.
- Prepare Crumble: In another bowl, mix flour, oats, brown sugar, and cinnamon. Add butter and use your fingers to mix until the mixture resembles coarse crumbs.
- Assemble: Place the raspberry mixture in the air fryer basket. Sprinkle the crumble mixture evenly over the raspberries.
- Air Fry: Preheat the air fryer to 350°F. Air fry the crumble for 15 minutes or until the topping is golden brown and the raspberries are bubbly.
- Serve: Serve warm, optionally topped with whipped cream or a scoop of vanilla ice cream.

Nutritional values per serving - Calories: 320 Fat: 12 g Sodium: 50 mg
Carbohydrates: 50 g Protein: 3 g

S'mores Dip

 5' 8' 4 Easy

Ingredients

✧ 1 cup milk chocolate chips
✧ 2 tablespoons heavy cream
✧ 1 cup mini marshmallows
✧ 4 graham crackers, broken into pieces for dipping

Ah, the s'mores dip—a delightful treat that reminds me of American campfires under starlit skies! It really captures the joy of sharing good food with loved ones. For an Italian twist, try drizzling a little espresso over the marshmallows before the final cook to add a subtle coffee flavor that enhances the chocolate beautifully.

Directions

✧ Prep Ingredients: In a suitable air fryer-safe dish, mix the chocolate chips with heavy cream.
✧ First Cook: Place the dish in the air fryer basket. Air fry at 360°F for about 3 minutes or until the chocolate is melted. Stir the chocolate until smooth.
✧ Add Marshmallows: Top the melted chocolate with mini marshmallows, covering the chocolate completely.
✧ Final Cook: Air fry at 360°F for another 5 minutes or until the marshmallows are golden brown and toasty.
✧ Serve: Serve immediately with graham crackers for dipping.

Nutritional values per serving - Calories: 280 Fat: 15 g Sodium: 60 mg Carbohydrates: 35 g Protein: 2 g

Stuffed Baked Apples

 10' 20'  4 Easy

Ingredients

✧ 4 large apples (such as Honeycrisp or Granny Smith)
✧ 1/4 cup chopped walnuts
✧ 1/4 cup dried cranberries or raisins
✧ 2 tablespoons brown sugar
✧ 1/2 teaspoon cinnamon
✧ 1/4 teaspoon nutmeg
✧ 1/4 cup rolled oats
✧ 2 tablespoons butter, melted
✧ 1/2 cup apple juice or water

In my youth, we often enjoyed simple fruit desserts, much like these stuffed apples, after a hearty meal. For a fun twist, try adding a splash of Amaretto to the filling before baking—it enhances the nutty flavor beautifully and brings a little Italian flair to this comforting dish!

Directions

✧ Prepare Apples: Core the apples, making a large well in the center and leaving the bottom intact.
✧ Mix Filling: In a bowl, combine walnuts, dried cranberries, brown sugar, cinnamon, nutmeg, and rolled oats. Stir in melted butter until the mixture is well coated.
✧ Stuff Apples: Spoon the filling into each apple, packing it tightly.
✧ Arrange for Cooking: Place the stuffed apples in the air fryer basket. Pour apple juice or water into the bottom of the basket to help create steam.
✧ Cook: Air fry at 350°F for 15-20 minutes, or until the apples are tender and the filling is bubbly.
✧ Serve Warm: Let cool slightly before serving, ideally with a dollop of vanilla ice cream or a drizzle of caramel sauce (Ch. 8)

Nutritional values per serving - Calories: 220 Fat: 8 g Sodium: 30 mg Carbohydrates: 38 g Protein: 2 g

Chapter 8: Mastering Homemade Basics

Buongiorno, my dear readers! Throughout this delightful journey of air frying and culinary exploration, we've touched upon many simple, yet flavor-packed recipes. Now, I feel a little spark in my heart urging me to share something very special with you. You see, as a retired chef who has spent a lifetime in the kitchens of sunny Italy, I have always cherished the art of creating from scratch. It's the soul of cooking!

I understand the modern world rushes us; we seek quicker paths, even in cooking, which leads many to the convenience of store-bought items. And yes, an air fryer is a marvelous tool for speeding things up without sacrificing quality. However, I invite you to occasionally slow down and savor the process of making your own basics. Whether it's a robust pesto, a zesty tomato sauce, or a simple breading, the magic of crafting these yourself is a rewarding experience.

In this chapter, I've compiled some essential recipes that serve as the foundation for many dishes in our book. It's my sincere hope that you'll find joy in these *little secrets* of the kitchen, enhancing not just the flavor of your meals, but also the connection to each dish you prepare. After all, cooking is not just about feeding the body but nourishing the soul. Let's embark on this beautiful endeavor together, hand in hand, with a sprinkle of chef's love!

Basic Risotto

 5'   20'   4   Easy

Directions

✧ Prepare Ingredients: In a large saucepan, melt 2 tablespoons of butter over medium heat. Add the chopped onion and sauté until translucent, about 3-4 minutes.
✧ Cook Rice: Add the Arborio rice to the pan and stir for 2 minutes to coat the rice grains with butter, allowing them to toast slightly without browning.
✧ Add Stock: Begin adding the warm stock, one ladle at a time, stirring frequently. Wait until each addition of stock is almost fully absorbed by the rice before adding the next ladle. Continue this process until the rice is creamy and al dente, which should take about 16-18 minutes.
✧ Finish with Cheese and Butter: Remove the pan from heat. Stir in the remaining 2 tablespoons of butter and the grated Parmigiano cheese. Season with salt and pepper to taste. Let the risotto rest for a minute to thicken slightly.
✧ Serve: Divide the risotto evenly among four plates, serve immediately.

Ingredients

✧ 1 1/2 cups Arborio rice
✧ 5 cups chicken or vegetable stock, kept warm
✧ 1/2 cup finely grated Parmigiano cheese
✧ 4 tablespoons unsalted butter
✧ 1 medium onion, finely chopped
✧ Salt to taste
✧ Freshly ground black pepper to taste

Nutritional values per serving - Calories: 450 Fat: 18 g Sodium: 600 mg Carbohydrates: 64 g Protein: 10 g

Boiled Octopus

 10' 60-90' 4 Easy

Ingredients

- ✧ 2 pounds octopus, cleaned
- ✧ 1 onion, halved
- ✧ 1 lemon, halved
- ✧ 2 bay leaves
- ✧ Salt to taste

Nutritional values per serving - Calories: 150 Fat: 2 g Sodium: 480 mg Carbohydrates: 8 g Protein: 25 g

Directions

- ✧ Prepare Octopus: Rinse the octopus under cold water. If it's not already cleaned, remove the beak and ink sac.
- ✧ Simmer: Fill a large pot with water, add the onion, lemon halves, bay leaves, and a pinch of salt. Bring to a boil.
- ✧ Cook Octopus: Once the water is boiling, submerge the octopus in the pot, reduce heat to low, and simmer. Cover the pot and cook until the octopus is tender, which can take between 60 to 90 minutes depending on the size of the octopus.
- ✧ Check Doneness: Test the octopus for doneness by piercing a tentacle with a fork; it should be tender and easy to puncture.
- ✧ Cool and Serve: Remove the octopus from the water and let it cool. It can now be sliced and used in various dishes, such as salads, grilled, or served with pasta.

Buffalo Sauce

 5' 5' 4 Easy

Ingredients

- ✧ 1/2 cup hot pepper sauce
- ✧ 1/3 cup unsalted butter
- ✧ 1 tablespoon white vinegar
- ✧ 1/4 teaspoon Worcestershire sauce
- ✧ 1/4 teaspoon cayenne pepper
- ✧ 1/8 teaspoon garlic powder

Nutritional values per serving - Calories: 140 Fat: 15 g Sodium: 750 mg Carbohydrates: 1 g Protein: 0 g

Directions

- ✧ Combine Ingredients: In a saucepan, combine the hot sauce, butter, vinegar, Worcestershire sauce, cayenne pepper, and garlic powder.
- ✧ Heat Sauce: Place the saucepan over medium heat and stir continuously until the butter is completely melted and the mixture is well combined, about 3 to 5 minutes.
- ✧ Simmer: Reduce the heat to low and simmer the sauce for a few minutes to blend the flavors. Season with salt to taste.
- ✧ Cool and Store: Remove from heat and let the sauce cool to room temperature. Transfer to an airtight container and refrigerate. Use as needed for coating wings, dressing burgers, or as a dip.

Caramel Sauce

 5' 10'  4* Easy

* about 1 cup total

Ingredients

- ✧ 1 cup granulated sugar
- ✧ 6 tablespoons unsalted butter, cut into pieces
- ✧ 1/2 cup heavy cream
- ✧ 1 teaspoon vanilla extract
- ✧ 1/4 teaspoon salt

Nutritional values per serving - Calories: 370 Fat: 23 g Sodium: 150 mg Carbohydrates: 40 g Protein: 1 g

Directions

- ✧ Melt Sugar: In a medium saucepan over medium heat, melt the sugar, stirring constantly with a heat-resistant spatula or wooden spoon. The sugar will form clumps but will eventually melt into a thick, amber-colored liquid as you continue to stir. Be careful not to burn it.
- ✧ Add Butter: Once the sugar is fully melted, add the butter pieces. Be careful as the caramel will bubble rapidly when the butter is added. Stir the butter into the caramel until it is completely melted, about 2 minutes.
- ✧ Pour in Heavy Cream: Very slowly, drizzle in the heavy cream while stirring. The mixture will rapidly bubble. After adding the cream, allow the mixture to boil for 1 minute. It will rise in the pan as it boils.
- ✧ Remove from Heat: Remove the pan from heat and stir in the vanilla extract and salt. Allow the caramel to cool down before using. It will thicken as it cools.
- ✧ Store: Pour the caramel into a glass jar and let it cool to room temperature, then store it in the refrigerator for up to 2 weeks. Warm before using if desired.

Ingredients

- ◇ 1 cup mayonnaise
- ◇ 2 chipotle peppers in adobo sauce, finely chopped
- ◇ 1 tablespoon adobo sauce (from the chipotle peppers can)
- ◇ 2 tablespoons lime juice
- ◇ 1 teaspoon lime zest
- ◇ 1/4 teaspoon salt
- ◇ 1/4 teaspoon garlic powder

Nutritional values per serving - Calories: 210 Fat: 22 g Sodium: 350 mg Carbohydrates: 2 g Protein: 0 g

Chipotle Lime Sauce

 5'   0'   4*   Easy

* about 1 cup total

Directions

- ◇ Mix Ingredients: In a medium bowl, combine all the ingredients: mayonnaise, chopped chipotle peppers, adobo sauce, lime juice, lime zest, salt, and garlic powder. Stir until well blended.
- ◇ Adjust Flavors: Taste and adjust the seasoning if necessary. Add more lime juice for extra tanginess or adobo sauce for more heat.
- ◇ Chill and Serve: Transfer the sauce to an airtight container and refrigerate for at least 30 minutes before serving to allow the flavors to meld. Serve chilled.

Chocolate Dipping Sauce

 5'   5'    4*   Easy

* about 1 cup total

Directions

- ◇ Heat Cream: In a small saucepan, heat the heavy cream over medium heat until it begins to simmer.
- ◇ Melt Chocolate: Remove the saucepan from heat and add the chocolate chips and butter, stirring until smooth and fully melted.
- ◇ Add Flavorings: Stir in the vanilla extract and a pinch of salt to enhance the flavors.
- ◇ Serve: Transfer the sauce to a serving bowl or container. Serve warm for dipping fruits, marshmallows, or pastries.

Ingredients

- ◇ 1/2 cup heavy cream
- ◇ 1 cup semi-sweet chocolate chips
- ◇ 1 tablespoon unsalted butter
- ◇ 1/2 teaspoon vanilla extract
- ◇ A pinch of salt

Nutritional values per serving - Calories: 260 Fat: 18 g Sodium: 40 mg Carbohydrates: 25 g Protein: 2 g

Cooked Beans

 8 hours*   1-2 hours   4   Easy

* including soaking

Ingredients

- ◇ 1 cup dried beans (such as black, pinto, or kidney)
- ◇ Water for soaking and cooking
- ◇ 1/2 teaspoon salt (optional)

Nutritional values per serving - Calories: 225 Fat: 1 g Sodium: 300 mg (if salted) Carbohydrates: 40 g Protein: 15 g

Directions

- ◇ Soak Beans: Rinse the dried beans under cold water to remove any debris. Place the beans in a large bowl and cover them with several inches of cold water. Let them soak overnight, or for at least 8 hours.
- ◇ Drain and Rinse: After soaking, drain the beans and rinse them again under cold water.
- ◇ Cook Beans: Transfer the soaked beans to a large pot and cover them with fresh water. Bring the water to a boil, reduce the heat, and simmer for 1 to 2 hours, or until the beans are tender. Add salt to the cooking water if desired, towards the end of cooking to enhance flavor without toughening the beans.
- ◇ Ready to Serve: Once the beans are cooked, drain them and they are ready to use in your recipes or to be stored for later use.

Cooked Chickpeas

 8 hours* 1-1,5 hours 4 Easy

* including soaking

Ingredients

✧ 1 cup dried chickpeas
✧ Water, for soaking and cooking
✧ 1/2 teaspoon salt (optional)

Directions

✧ Soak Chickpeas: Place the chickpeas in a large bowl and cover them with water, allowing for about 2-3 inches of water above the chickpeas. Soak them overnight or for at least 8 hours to hydrate and soften.
✧ Drain and Rinse: After soaking, drain the chickpeas and rinse them thoroughly under cold water.
✧ Cook Chickpeas: Transfer the soaked chickpeas to a large pot and cover them with fresh water by several inches. Add salt if using. Bring to a boil, then reduce the heat to a simmer.
✧ Simmer: Let the chickpeas cook for 1 to 1.5 hours, or until they are tender and fully cooked. The cooking time may vary depending on the age and size of the chickpeas.
✧ Drain: Once cooked, drain the chickpeas and use them immediately, or store them in the refrigerator for up to a week.

Nutritional values per serving - Calories: 269 Fat: 4 g Sodium: 300 mg (if salted) Carbohydrates: 45 g Protein: 14 g

Cooked Quinoa

 5' 15' 4 Easy

Ingredients

✧ 1 cup quinoa
✧ 2 cups water or broth (for enhanced flavor)
✧ 1/4 teaspoon salt (optional)

Nutritional values per serving - Calories: 156 Fat: 3 g Sodium: 150 mg (if broth is used) Carbohydrates: 27 g Protein: 6 g

Directions

✧ Rinse Quinoa: Place the quinoa in a fine-mesh sieve and rinse under cold water for a minute to remove the saponin coating, which can make it taste bitter.
✧ Cook Quinoa: In a medium saucepan, combine the rinsed quinoa, water or broth, and salt. Bring to a boil over high heat.
✧ Simmer: Reduce the heat to low, cover, and simmer until the quinoa is tender and the liquid is absorbed, about 15 minutes.
✧ Rest: Remove from heat and let the quinoa sit covered for 5 minutes. This allows it to become fluffy.
✧ Fluff and Serve: Fluff the quinoa gently with a fork before serving or using in other recipes.

Easy Pizza Dough

 15' 1 hour*  4** Easy

* rising time   ** makes 2 medium pizzas

Ingredients

✧ 2 1/4 teaspoons (1 packet) active dry yeast
✧ 1 teaspoon sugar
✧ 1 cup warm water (110°F to 115°F)
✧ 2 1/2 cups all-purpose flour, plus extra for dusting
✧ 1 teaspoon salt
✧ 2 tablespoons olive oil

Directions

✧ Activate Yeast: In a small bowl, dissolve the sugar and yeast in warm water. Let it sit for 5 minutes until the mixture is frothy, indicating that the yeast is active.
✧ Combine Dry Ingredients: In a large mixing bowl, whisk together the flour and salt.
✧ Add Wet Ingredients: Make a well in the center of the flour mixture and pour in the yeast mixture and olive oil. Mix until a shaggy dough forms.
✧ Knead the Dough: Turn the dough out onto a floured surface and knead for about 5-7 minutes, until smooth and elastic. Add more flour as needed to prevent sticking.
✧ Let it Rise: Place the dough in a greased bowl, cover it with a clean towel, and let it rise in a warm place for about 1 hour, or until it has doubled in size.
✧ Prepare for Use: Once risen, punch down the dough, then divide it into 2 equal parts for pizza bases. Roll out as needed for your pizza recipes.

Nutritional values per serving - Calories: 287 Fat: 5 g Sodium: 600 mg Carbohydrates: 51 g Protein: 7 g

Italian Breadcrumbs

 10' 15' 4* 👨‍🍳 Easy

*about 2 cups total

Ingredients

✧ 4 cups of day-old bread, cubed (use a crusty Italian or French loaf for best results)
✧ 2 tablespoons olive oil
✧ 1 teaspoon garlic powder
✧ 1 teaspoon dried parsley
✧ 1/2 teaspoon dried oregano
✧ 1/2 teaspoon dried basil
✧ 1/4 teaspoon salt

Nutritional values per serving - Calories: 150 Fat: 7 g Sodium: 200 mg Carbohydrates: 18 g Protein: 4 g

Directions

✧ Preheat Oven: Preheat your oven to 300°F.
✧ Prepare Bread: Spread the bread cubes on a baking sheet in a single layer.
✧ Toast Bread: Bake in the preheated oven for 10-15 minutes, or until the bread is dry and slightly golden. Stir occasionally to ensure even toasting.
✧ Season and Blend: Let the toasted bread cool slightly. Transfer to a food processor, add olive oil, garlic powder, parsley, oregano, basil, and salt. Pulse until the mixture reaches a fine, crumbly texture.
✧ Store or Use: Use immediately, or store in an airtight container for up to 2 weeks.

Lemon Curd

 5' 10' 4* 👨‍🍳 Easy

*about 2 cups total

Ingredients

✧ 3/4 cup fresh lemon juice (about 3-4 lemons)
✧ 1 tablespoon lemon zest
✧ 1 cup sugar
✧ 3 large eggs
✧ 1/2 cup unsalted butter, cubed

Nutritional values per 1/4 cup - Calories: 200 Fat: 12 g Sodium: 20 mg Carbohydrates: 22 g Protein: 2 g

Directions

✧ Mix Ingredients: In a medium saucepan, whisk together lemon juice, lemon zest, sugar, and eggs.
✧ Cook: Add the butter to the saucepan and cook over medium-low heat, stirring constantly, until the butter is melted and the mixture is thick enough to coat the back of a spoon, about 10 minutes.
✧ Strain: Remove from heat and strain the mixture through a fine mesh sieve into a bowl to remove any lumps and the zest.
✧ Cool and Store: Allow the lemon curd to cool to room temperature. Cover with plastic wrap, pressing the wrap directly onto the surface of the curd to prevent a skin from forming. Refrigerate until fully chilled and set, about 2 hours. Store in the refrigerator for up to a week or freeze for longer storage.

Marinara Sauce

 5' 20' 4* 👨‍🍳 Easy

*about 4 cups total

Ingredients

✧ 2 tablespoons olive oil
✧ 1 small onion, finely chopped
✧ 3 cloves garlic, minced
✧ 1 (28-ounce) can crushed tomatoes
✧ 1 teaspoon dried oregano
✧ 1 teaspoon dried basil
✧ 1/2 teaspoon sugar
✧ Salt and pepper to taste

Nutritional values per 1/2 cup - Calories: 70 Fat: 4 g Sodium: 300 mg Carbohydrates: 9 g Protein: 2 g

Directions

✧ Sauté Onions and Garlic: In a large saucepan, heat the olive oil over medium heat. Add the chopped onion and cook until translucent, about 5 minutes. Add the minced garlic and cook for another minute until fragrant.
✧ Add Tomatoes and Seasonings: Stir in the crushed tomatoes, oregano, basil, and sugar. Season with salt and pepper.
✧ Simmer: Bring the sauce to a simmer and reduce the heat to low. Let it simmer gently for 15 minutes, stirring occasionally.
✧ Taste and Adjust: Taste the sauce and adjust the seasoning if necessary. If the sauce is too acidic, a little more sugar can be added to balance the flavors.

Mint Chutney

 10' 0' 4* Easy

* about 1 cup total

Ingredients

- ✧ 1 cup fresh mint leaves, packed
- ✧ 1/2 cup fresh cilantro leaves, packed
- ✧ 1 green chili, seeded and chopped (adjust based on heat preference)
- ✧ 2 tablespoons lemon juice
- ✧ 1 teaspoon sugar
- ✧ 1/2 teaspoon salt
- ✧ 2 tablespoons water, or as needed to blend
- ✧ 1 tablespoon yogurt (optional, for creaminess)

Nutritional values per tablespoon - Calories: 5 Fat: 0 g Sodium: 75 mg Carbohydrates: 1 g Protein: 0 g

Directions

- ✧ Blend Ingredients: In a blender or food processor, combine the mint leaves, cilantro, green chili, lemon juice, sugar, salt, and water. Blend until smooth. If the mixture is too thick, add a little more water until you achieve the desired consistency.
- ✧ Add Yogurt: If using yogurt, blend it into the chutney for a creamy texture.
- ✧ Taste and Adjust: Taste the chutney and adjust the seasoning or acidity as needed.

Pesto Genovese

 10' 0' 4* Easy

* about 1 cup total

Ingredients

- ✧ 2 cups fresh basil leaves, packed
- ✧ 1/3 cup pine nuts
- ✧ 2 large garlic cloves, peeled
- ✧ 1/2 cup extra virgin olive oil
- ✧ 1/2 cup grated Parmigiano cheese
- ✧ Salt to taste

Nutritional values per tablespoon - Calories: 100 Fat: 10 g Sodium: 75 mg Carbohydrates: 1 g Protein: 2 g

Directions

- ✧ Prepare Ingredients: Wash the basil leaves gently and pat them dry with a paper towel. Make sure they are completely dry before using.
- ✧ Blend Dry Ingredients: In a food processor, combine basil leaves, pine nuts, and garlic. Pulse until everything is finely chopped.
- ✧ Add Oil: With the processor running, slowly pour in the olive oil and process until the mixture is smooth.
- ✧ Mix in Cheese: Add the grated Parmigiano cheese and pulse a few times to mix thoroughly into the pesto.
- ✧ Season: Taste the pesto and add salt as needed, blending again to mix it in.

Ranch Dressing

 5' 0' 4* Easy

* about 1 cup total

Ingredients

- ✧ 1/2 cup mayonnaise
- ✧ 1/2 cup sour cream
- ✧ 1/4 cup buttermilk
- ✧ 1 tablespoon fresh chives, finely chopped
- ✧ 1 tablespoon fresh parsley, finely chopped
- ✧ 1 clove garlic, minced
- ✧ 1/2 teaspoon dried dill
- ✧ 1/2 teaspoon onion powder
- ✧ 1/4 teaspoon salt
- ✧ 1/4 teaspoon black pepper

Nutritional values per tablespoon - Calories: 60 Fat: 6 g Sodium: 80 mg Carbohydrates: 1 g Protein: 1 g

Directions

- ✧ Combine Ingredients: In a medium bowl, whisk together mayonnaise, sour cream, and buttermilk until smooth.
- ✧ Add Herbs and Seasonings: Stir in chives, parsley, minced garlic, dried dill, onion powder, salt, and black pepper.
- ✧ Mix Well: Mix thoroughly to ensure all ingredients are well combined.
- ✧ Chill: Refrigerate the dressing for at least 30 minutes before serving to allow flavors to meld together.

Tartar Sauce

 10' 0' 4* Easy

* about 1 cup total

Ingredients

- ✧ 1 cup mayonnaise
- ✧ 3 tablespoons pickles (dill or sweet), finely chopped
- ✧ 1 tablespoon capers, finely chopped
- ✧ 1 tablespoon fresh lemon juice
- ✧ 1 teaspoon Dijon mustard
- ✧ 1 tablespoon fresh parsley, finely chopped
- ✧ Salt and pepper, to taste

Nutritional values per tablespoon - Calories: 100 Fat: 10 g Sodium: 120 mg Carbohydrates: 1 g Protein: 0 g

Directions

- ✧ Mix Ingredients: In a small bowl, combine mayonnaise, chopped pickles, capers, lemon juice, Dijon mustard, and chopped parsley.
- ✧ Season: Add salt and pepper to taste and stir well to combine all ingredients thoroughly.
- ✧ Chill and Serve: Refrigerate for at least 30 minutes before serving to allow flavors to meld together.

Tomato Sauce

 5' 30'  4* Easy

* about 2 cups total

Ingredients

- ✧ 2 tablespoons olive oil
- ✧ 1 small onion, finely chopped
- ✧ 2 garlic cloves, minced
- ✧ 1 (28-ounce) can of whole peeled tomatoes
- ✧ 1 teaspoon dried oregano
- ✧ 1 teaspoon dried basil
- ✧ Salt and pepper, to taste

Nutritional values per 1/4 cup - Calories: 70 Fat: 5 g Sodium: 290 mg Carbohydrates: 6 g Protein: 1 g

Directions

- ✧ fragrant.
- ✧ Simmer Tomatoes: Pour in the whole peeled tomatoes, including the juice from the can. Crush the tomatoes with the back of a spoon. Stir in oregano and basil. Season with salt and pepper.
- ✧ Cook: Bring the sauce to a simmer and reduce heat to low. Let it cook, uncovered, for about 25 minutes, stirring occasionally, until the sauce thickens.
- ✧ Blend (Optional): For a smoother sauce, use an immersion blender to blend the sauce directly in the pan until the desired consistency is reached.

Yogurt Dipping Sauce

 5' 0' 4* Easy

* about 1 cup total

Ingredients

- ✧ 1 cup plain Greek yogurt
- ✧ 1 tablespoon lemon juice
- ✧ 1 garlic clove, minced
- ✧ 1 tablespoon chopped fresh dill
- ✧ Salt and pepper, to taste

Nutritional values per serving - Calories: 45 Fat: 1 g Sodium: 30 mg Carbohydrates: 3 g Protein: 6 g

Directions

- ✧ Combine Ingredients: In a small bowl, mix together the Greek yogurt, lemon juice, minced garlic, and chopped dill. Stir until well combined.
- ✧ Season: Season with salt and pepper to taste. Adjust the seasoning and herbs according to your preference.
- ✧ Chill: For best flavor, cover and refrigerate for at least 30 minutes before serving to allow the flavors to meld.

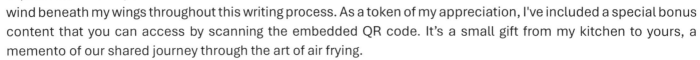

CONCLUSION AND BONUS CONTENT

As I draw the final lines of this culinary journey through air frying, my heart is full of gratitude and my kitchen, still fragrant with the myriad aromas we've explored together. At this juncture, I must extend my deepest thanks to those who have made this book not only possible but a true labor of love.

First, to my dear niece, Elisabetta, a young soul with a passion for flavors and the true instigator of this adventure. It was she who, one Christmas, asked for an air fryer as a gift. Little did she know, this simple request would lead her old uncle to pen these pages. Elisabetta, may your culinary path be as rich and rewarding as the meals we've shared. Here's to your future, which I trust will be as brilliant and inspiring as you are.

A heartfelt thank you to Martina Torri, our esteemed nutritionist and co-author. Martina, your expertise in weaving through the nutritional intricacies has been indispensable. Your dedication ensures that our creations are not only delightful but also nourishing, providing our readers with food that is as good for the body as it is for the soul.

I must also tip my chef's hat to my good friend, Chef Takis Papadopoulos. Takis, your contributions have imbued our Greek recipes with authenticity and your spirited guidance has brought a piece of Greece into our kitchens. Thank you for making our dishes genuinely Greek and for sharing your culinary wisdom so generously.

And to you, my loyal readers, who have accompanied me on this flavorful expedition—thank you. Your enthusiasm and feedback have been the wind beneath my wings throughout this writing process. As a token of my appreciation, I've included a special bonus content that you can access by scanning the embedded QR code. It's a small gift from my kitchen to yours, a memento of our shared journey through the art of air frying.

From my heart to your table, *buon appetito* and may your meals always bring you joy!

Chef Claudio

24094265R00044